Aircraft
OF THE ACES
Legends of the Skies

Featuring the acclaimed artwork
of Iain Wyllie and Mark Postlethwaite

Aircraft
OF THE ACES
Legends of the Skies

*Featuring the acclaimed artwork
of Iain Wyllie and Mark Postlethwaite*

Compiled by Tony Holmes

Foreword by Generalleutnant Günther Rall a.D.

First published in Great Britain in 2004
by Osprey Publishing
1st Floor, Elms Court, Chapel Way
Botley, Oxford, OX2 9LP

A CIP catalogue record for this book is available from the British Library

ISBN 1 84176 825 1

Written and Edited by Tony Holmes
Page design by Mark Holt
Cover Artwork by Mark Postlethwaite
Cover paintings in Chapters 8 and 12 by Keith Woodcock
Aircraft Profiles by John Weal, Chris Davey, Harry Dempsey,
Richard Caruana, Mark Rolfe and Jim Laurier
Index by Alan Thatcher
Originated by Grasmere Digital Imaging, Leeds, UK
Printed and bound by L-Rex Printing Company Ltd

04 05 06 07 08   10 9 8 7 6 5 4 3 2 1

EDITOR'S NOTE
To make the best-selling *Aircraft of the Aces* series as authoritative as possible,
the editor would be interested in hearing from any individual who may have
relevant photographs, documentation or first-hand experiences relating to
aircrews, and their aircraft, of the various theatres of war. Any material used
will be credited to its original source. Please write to Tony Holmes via
e-mail at:

tony.holmes@osprey-jets.freeserve.co.uk

ACKNOWLEDGEMENTS
Firstly, the author would like to thank Generalleutnant Günther Rall
a.D. for supplying the foreword which so accurately sets the scene
for the book. Thank you also to Elke and John Weal for their
assistance in facilitating the production of the foreword. I am also
greatly indebted to the following individuals for supplying words
and photos for this volume at very short notice; Jiri Rajlich, John
Stanaway, George Mellinger, William Hess, Norman Franks, John
Weal, Greg Van Wyngarden, Jon Guttman, Christopher Shores,
Andrew Thomas, Giorgio Apostolo, Terrill Clements, Carl
Molesworth, Boris Ciglic, György Punka, Dénes Bernad, Shlomo
Aloni and Warren Thompson

For a catalogue of all titles published by Osprey Military and Aviation please write to:

Osprey Direct UK, PO Box 140,
Wellingborough, Northants NN8 4ZA, UK
E-mail: **info@ospreydirect.co.uk**

Osprey Direct USA, c/o MBI Publishing, PO Box 1,
729 Prospect Ave, Osceola, WI 54020, USA
E-mail: **info@ospreydirectusa.com**

Visit Osprey at **www.ospreypublishing.com**

CONTENTS

FOREWORD

In World War 1, aircraft were initially regarded as little more than a novelty. As the conflict progressed, they grew in numbers and importance. But aviation was not a decisive factor in determining the outcome of that war. By World War 2 the situation had changed dramatically. Aviation technology had advanced, and the quality and quantity of the machines equipping the world's air arms meant that the aircraft had become a decisive weapon of war, both tactically and strategically.

Fighters played an integral part and essential role in every campaign by:

- gaining and maintaining local air superiority
- providing escorts for bombers
- carrying out reconnaissance missions
- flying ground-attack sorties in support of the armies in the field

But circumstances and conditions varied widely from theatre to theatre. In the west during the Battle of Britain, in which I served as *Staffelkapitän* of 8./JG 52, the Royal Air Force achieved air superiority through excellent leadership – both from the ground and in the air – and from the technical quality of their equipment, in particular the Spitfire and Hurricane. And without control of England's skies, a German invasion proved impossible.

On the eastern front, where we in III./JG 52 fought in the southern sector, it was a war of continual movement. I changed bases no fewer than 44 times between 1942 and 1944, with sites for new fields often being reconnoitred and selected from the air. The logistical problems were enormous, as there were no roads for the transfer of heavy technical machinery. And the atrocious weather only made matters worse, with temperatures in the winter months dropping as low as 40(!) degrees below zero.

This environment imposed severe physical and psychological pressures upon the pilots, whose living conditions were at best primitive. From April to October we often lived in tents on the open fields which served as our bases, while in the winter we were housed in dug-outs or old abandoned farm buildings. By contrast, pilots in the west usually had permanent, and comfortable, pre-war quarters to which they could return after operations.

The conduct of the war in the west, in the air and on the ground, was generally fair and correct – one might almost say chivalrous. In the east it could be savage and brutal. I lost many friends and comrades who were forced down unhurt behind enemy lines, captured by the Soviets and never seen again.

After my posting back to Germany in the spring of 1944 as *Gruppenkommandeur* of II./JG 11, I experienced for the first time the heavy US daylight bomber raids and the full might of the Allies' strategic air supremacy.

On 12 May 1944 I led my *Gruppe* against 800 bombers, escorted by P-51, P-47 and P-38 long-range fighters. We did not stand a chance. But the Luftwaffe's outnumbered *Jagdflieger* continued to fly and fight despite their inevitable heavy losses. None of us thought in terms of final victory any more. Our one concern was the protection of Germany's cities, and the people living in them.

But these are now *tempi passati*. Sixty years after the end of a global war, we – that is, the fighter pilots who took part in it and survived – have come to respect each other's commitments and sacrifices. Among one-time opponents there are now many bonds of friendship.

And the choice of paintings selected for this second volume of *Aircraft of the Aces*, depicting the actions of fighter pilots of many nations over many decades, is a perfect example of that very sentiment:

'Yesterday's enemies, today's friends!'

Günther Rall
Generalleutnant a.D.
Bad Reichenhall, June 2004

'NAVAL 1' ACE

'Several Huns put themselves in our path, but we were cute and accepted not of their kind offer, till one, not knowing the sting in the "Tripod", fell victim to his horrid ways.'

Royal Naval Air Service (RNAS) Flight Commander Roderic S Dallas DSC of 1 Naval Squadron flew Sopwith Triplane N5436 between late January and May 1917, achieving ten victories with the fighting scout. After his first flight in this particular machine, he recorded in his log-book;

'Tested oxygen set and went up to 26,000 ft – very curious sensation. I got drunk with the oxygen and could hardly recognise the country below me. I was frost bitten when coming down, and got it badly. This is the height record for the Triplane.'

The future second-ranking Australian ace, Dallas' first victory (an LVG C observation aircraft) in N5436 came on 1 February 1917, shortly after his unit had moved up to the frontline to support the beleaguered Royal Flying Corps (RFC). He did not score again until 5 April, by which time 1 Naval Squadron had commenced operations in the build up to the Battle of Arras (launched four days later). Dallas fought with a formidable Albatros scout on this eve of battle patrol, and the action is depicted opposite. The Australian ace described the engagement in his log-book;

'We start the big show properly, and everybody is indeed a little anxious to see what things are really like. I led the formation, Teddy (Gerrard) being good enough to come with me. As we

Queenslander Roderic S Dallas poses for the camera in his distinctive RNAS uniform while undergoing training in late 1915 (*via Norman Franks*)

Triplane pilots of 1 Naval Squadron pose for a group photograph at Bailleul aerodrome in July 1917. They are, from left to right, S M Kinkead DSC (6 kills on Triplanes and 35 overall), J H Forman (1 kill on Triplanes and 9 overall), H Wallace, A G A Spence (6 kills on Triplanes and 9 overall), H L Everitt, H V Rowley (5 kills on Triplanes and 9 overall), Luard, Magrath, E D Crundell (3 kills on Triplanes and 7 overall), W H Sneath, Burton, A R McAfee, S W Rosevear (8 kills on Triplanes and 25 overall), R P Minifie (17 kills on Triplanes and 21 overall), R S Dallas (16 kills on Triplanes and 32 overall), C B Ridley (4 kills on Triplanes and 11 overall), J S deWilde, White and E B Holden (*via Norman Franks*)

climbed towards the lines, we felt secure, and were proud of our mounts. We soon got intimation that "Fritz" dwelt below, for from our high and lofty position we could look down with scorn on our baffled pursuers. Several Huns put themselves in our path, but we were cute and accepted not of their kind offer, till one, not knowing the sting in the "Tripod", fell victim to his horrid ways. We landed at Ham short of gas.'

Again flying Triplane N5436, Dallas claimed a Albatros D II scout 'out of control' in this action, the aircraft falling earthwards east of St Quentin at noon. He destroyed two more Albatros scouts (this time newer D IIIs) on 22 April, as he recounted in his log-book;

'Big scrap – met the "Travelling Circus" – and (Tom) Culling, my valiant comrade in the air, went with me into a formation of 14 of them. We revved around and counter-attacked, so to speak, and in the general mix-up Culling got one and I got two'.

Such was the significance of the action on the 22nd that it was reported in the official Royal Air Force (RAF) publication that charted the history of aerial combat in World War 1, *The War in the Air;*

'The Sopwith pilots Flt Cdr R S Dallas and Flt Sub-Lt T G Culling met an enemy formation of 14 two-seaters and single-seat

Following initial Admiralty testing at RNAS Chingford, in Essex, prototype Sopwith Triplane N500 was sent on trial to 'A' Squadron, 1 Naval Wing, in Dunkirk in June 1916, where it was used by Australian R S Dallas in combat. The machine was also flown by other naval pilots who were keen to gain experience on the type. The scout was supplied to the RNAS in factory finish, including distinctive reflective underwing doping, which shows up clearly in this photograph (*via Norman Franks*)

fighters. The German pilots were flying towards the lines at 16,000 ft on a mission that appeared to be of some importance, but they were frustrated by the Sopwiths which fought the Germans for 45 minutes, kept their formation split up, shot three of them down – one fell in flames and one crashed – and left the remainder only when the Germans had retreated, individually and at low height, far to the east.'

For his part in this action, Dallas was Mentioned in Dispatches once again, and awarded the coveted *Croix de Guerre* by the French.

PILOT BIOGRAPHY – RODERIC S DALLAS

Born on 30 June 1891 in Mount Stanley, Queensland, Stan Dallas joined the Australian Army in 1913 and received a commission several months later. Following the outbreak of World War 1 in August 1914, he applied for a transfer to the RFC in the UK but was rejected. Unperturbed, Dallas then approached the Royal Navy, and was duly accepted by the RNAS. Commencing flying training in June 1915, he had his wings by November and joined 1 Naval Wing in Dunkirk on 3 December. Piloting two-seaters and single-seat Nieuport 11 *Bébé* scouts on reconnaissance patrols over the North Sea, often in terrible weather, Dallas' flying abilities rapidly developed to the point where he claimed his first three combat victories in April and May 1916 flying the diminutive French *Bébé*.

Sub-Lt Dallas officially achieved 'acedom' in the prototype Sopwith Triplane N500 on 9 July 1916 when he sent a Fokker E III down 'out of control' over Mariakerke. By February 1917 his score stood at seven, he had been awarded the Distinguished Service Cross and he was now a flight commander in the newly-established 1 Naval Squadron (formerly 1 Naval Wing). With the unit now fully equipped with Triplanes, it was sent to the Somme front in April to help hard-pressed RFC squadrons deal with the Fokker 'scourge'. Dallas made the most of this opportunity by claiming eight victories between 5 and 30 April, followed by two more in May.

Given command of 'Naval 1' on 14 June, with his official score then standing at 17 victories, Dallas had boosted his tally to 23 by the time he left the unit in March 1918 – having flown Camels during his final eight months with 'Naval 1', Dallas became a SE 5a pilot when he was made CO of the RAF's No 40 Sqn in early April.

On 1 June 1918, with his overall score having reached 32 (some sources claim that it could be as high as 56), Dallas took off alone on a mid-morning patrol over the frontline. Flying west of the Allied trenches, he was attacked out of the clouds by a trio of Fokker Dr I triplanes from *Jasta* 14. Australia's second-ranking ace was fatally wounded when shots fired by *Staffelführer* Leutnant Johannes Werner hit the cockpit of his SE 5a, and he crashed to his death near Lievin – Dallas was Werner's sixth of seven victims.

SPECIFICATION

Sopwith Triplane

TYPE:	single-seat, single-engined triplane fighter
ACCOMMODATION:	pilot
DIMENSIONS:	length 18 ft 10 in (5.74 m) wingspan 26 ft 6 in (8.08 m) height 10 ft 6 in (3.20 m)
WEIGHTS:	empty 993 lb (450 kg) maximum take-off 1415 lb (642 kg)
PERFORMANCE:	maximum speed 116 mph (187 kmh) range, endurance of 2.75 hours powerplant Clerget 9B output 130 hp (96.6 kW)
ARMAMENT:	one (some with two) fixed Vickers 0.303-in machine gun immediately forward of the cockpit
FIRST FLIGHT DATE:	28 May 1916
OPERATORS:	UK, France
PRODUCTION:	150

Built as a replacement for the Pup, and boasting a fuselage similar to its famous forebear, the Triplane boasted a superior rate of climb and greatly improved manoeuvrability thanks to its extra wing. Indeed, when the type made its combat debut with the RNAS in late 1916, the Triplane could easily out-climb any other aircraft operated by either side over the Western Front. Aside from its use by the RNAS, the Triplane was also due to serve with the RFC, but a deal struck in February 1917 saw the Navy exchange all its SPAD VIIs for all the Triplanes then on order for the RFC. This agreement subsequently resulted in the planned production run for the Triplane being rapidly scaled back, and only 150 were completed. Nevertheless, the design had a great impact when it finally met the enemy – so much so that the German High Command immediately ordered their manufacturers to produce triplane designs to counter the Sopwith fighter, the most famous of which was the Fokker Dr I. Aside from the Triplane's use by the RNAS, 16 examples were also supplied to the French Navy in mid 1917. Naval squadrons on the Western Front began replacing their well used Triplanes with Camels from July 1917 onwards, and the last examples in frontline service were flown by Home Defence units in southern England.

Triplane N5436 'C' of Sub-Lt Roderic Dallas, 1 Naval Squadron, La Bellevue, France, April 1917

Australian ace Roderic Stanley Dallas of 'Naval 1' flew this aircraft between December 1916 and May 1917, during which time he used it to claim 11 victories. Future ace C B Ridley then flew the veteran fighter in August and September 1917, scoring a further two victories with it. Very much a 'plain Jane' Triplane, it had a metal cowling and a clear-doped fin and wheel covers.

LAST VICTORY WITH *JASTA* 2

'I stayed behind him almost continuously, and could get off good bursts at the closest distance.'

The great ace Werner Voss watches an aircraft being demonstrated alongside legendary fighting scout designer Anthony Fokker. Voss, with his 'Blue Max' worn around his neck, would soon claim his final kills in an early pre-production example of Fokker's famous triplane scout (*via Greg VanWyngarden*)

The mercurial Werner Voss first saw fighter action with *Jasta* 2 Boelcke from late 1916 through to May 1917. During this period he achieved 28 victories, despite being away from the front in April 1917 – a time during which the RFC lost its greatest number of aeroplanes. Iain Wyllie's painting depicts the action fought over the Western Front on 9 May 1917 by Voss and 2Lt George Hadrill of No 54 Sqn, who was flying a Sopwith Pup. The latter pilot lost out in this engagement, being forced down behind German lines, where he was captured. Hadrill represented Voss's 27th aerial success, the downing of the Pup being the second of three victories claimed by the ace in this, his final day of action with *Jasta* 2. He would add 20 more victories before being killed in combat four months later.

Unlike a number of his contemporaries, very few of Voss' written combat reports survive. Indeed, there is not one for the action represented in this artwork. However, Voss did produce a detailed report following his success of 18 March 1917, when he shot down BE 2d 5770 of Capt G S Thorne (pilot) and 2Lt P E H Van Baerle (observer) of No 13 Sqn RFC for his 19th victory. This fight became quite famous in the propaganda literature of the 1930s, and Voss' original combat report was preserved by the German author Rolf Italiaander in his biography of Voss, *Pour le Mérite Flieger mit 20 Jahren* (published by G Weise of Berlin in 1939). It was Voss' second victory of the day, the ace having just

shot down BE 2e 5784 of No 8 Sqn at 1840 hrs. Voss climbed away from this victory, and only ten minutes later he attacked BE 2d 5770. The German ace's combat account read – translated by O'Brien Browne – as follows;

'Report from Leutnant Voss about the shooting down of a BE biplane two-seater on 18/3/1917, around 6.50 in the afternoon near Boyelles. Two MGs (machine guns) are with the 1st Komp. (company) of the IR 107 (*Infanterie Regiment* 107). Aircraft set on fire by me. Aircraft number 5770.

'While I was continually spiralling upwards over Neuville together with Leutnant Wortmann, who was always behind me, a BE two-seater came towards us somewhat to the north and much higher than we were, and then continued in a southerly direction. As I later determined, he was engaged in artillery spotting.

'I had soon reached the height of the BE, and approached closer to him from behind. Some 200 metres behind me was Leutnant Wortmann, and quite farther away the remaining machines (of his *Staffel*) were also following.

'The opponent shot at me from a distance of about 200 metres and dove steeply back to his Front. Because of my continual fire,

which I began at about 100 metres distance, and which I held until I was right behind him, the BE went into banks and spirals. I stayed behind him almost continuously, and could get off good bursts at the closest distance. After I had followed him down with many bankings, suddenly a second Albatros from my *Staffel* dove in between us from the left, and a crash almost happened. The Albatros turned upwards once more while I followed the opponent all the way down till right over the earth, and shot at him. During an emergency landing, the BE (5770) got quite smashed up.

'I recognised the cavalrymen running about by their steel helmets and field caps to be Germans, and so I decided to land on a grassy area laying nearby. Here, I discovered these cavalrymen were the last Germans before the advancing enemy, whose own patrol was staying close by. I took out the two Lewis machine guns from the aeroplane and had them brought back to the First Company of IR 107, and to be stored there. I shot one of the gas tanks of the BE, set it on fire and then took off again.'

Werner Voss used this distinctively marked Albatros D III while flying with both *Jastas* 2 and 5 in 1917. The ace and his aircraft were photographed just prior to their controversial posting to *Jasta* 5 on 20 May 1917. Voss' score stood at 28 victories at the time (*via Greg VanWyngarden*)

Werner Voss (left) poses with his parents and his younger brother Max at Eglesburg during his *Pour le Merite* leave in early April 1917 (*via Greg VanWyngarden*)

PILOT BIOGRAPHY – WERNER VOSS

Werner Voss was born in Krefeld on 13 April 1887. When he was 27, he enlisted in his local militia, then went to war with the 2. Westfälische Husaren Regiment Nr 11 – a unit known as the 'dancing hussars'. Like so many other cavalrymen, the stalemate of trench warfare failed to meet his expectations, and he transferred into aviation in August 1915. Once trained, Voss was assigned to *Kasta* 20 of *Kagohl* IV, and he began his career as a pilot in the Verdun area. He was happily transferred to *Jasta* Boelcke on 21 November 1916, and opened his account with two victories six days later.

Voss scored rapidly in February and March 1917, and on the 17th of the latter month he received the Knight's Cross with Swords of the Royal Hohenzollern House Order (the 'Hohenzollern'). With his tally at 24, he received the 'Blue Max' on 8 April. This was followed by routine leave, during which Voss missed most of the killing time of 'Bloody April'. In May 1917 he returned to *Jasta* Boelcke and brought his score to 28 (12 of them being hapless BE 2s), but the young fighter ace – he had just turned 20 – was dissatisfied with his *Staffelführer*, the veteran Hauptmann Franz Walz. Along with another misguided young pilot, Werner Voss submitted charges to his superiors that Walz was 'war-weary', and that an elite unit like *Jasta* Boelcke required a more dynamic leader. Their blatant disregard for the military code of conduct and the chain of command saw both pilots posted out of the prestigious *Jasta*. Voss received a severe, but private, reprimand, his youth and record saving him from harsher punishment.

Voss was given acting command of *Jasta* 5 on 20 May, then a scant nine days later he moved to *Jasta* 29. His time as *Staffelführer* only lasted five days, whereupon he went to command *Jasta* 14. Voss seems to have cared little for the responsibilities of command, and despised paperwork. At the end of July 1917 his old comrade Manfred von Richthofen called upon him to take command of *Jasta* 10, and Voss was soon building up the score of this previously lacklustre unit. Issued with one of the first Fokker F I triplanes to reach the front in early September 1917, Voss saw considerable action in the machine up until his death in action in the storied clash with seven SE 5as of the crack No 56 Sqn on 23 September 1917. Aged just 20, Voss had been credited with 48 victories prior to his death.

Albatros D III of Leutnant Werner Voss, *Jasta* 2 Boelcke and Jasta 5, mid-1917
Werner Voss, during his period with *Jasta* Boelcke, flew this much-decorated Albatros D III. When interviewed by historian Alex Imrie (circa 1960), Voss' motor mechanic Karl Timm recalled that the ace instructed him and Flieger Christian Rüser (the airframe mechanic) to paint a red heart with white border on both sides of the fuselage, and there are photos of Voss himself touching up the white border. Then Voss had them add a white swastika (merely a good luck symbol at this time). Timm told Voss he thought this looked a bit bare, and suggested that he add a laurel wreath around the swastika, which the pilot agreed to. Voss continued to fly this D III in these markings at *Jasta* 5, but it almost certainly did not follow him to *Jasta* 10.

SPECIFICATION

Albatros D III

TYPE:	single-seat, single-engined biplane fighter
ACCOMMODATION:	pilot
DIMENSIONS:	length 24 ft 0 in (7.33 m) wingspan 29 ft 8 in (9.04 m) height 9 ft 9.25 in (2.98 m)
WEIGHTS:	empty 1457 lb (661 kg) maximum take-off 1953 lb (886 kg)
PERFORMANCE:	maximum speed 107 mph (180 kmh) range 217 miles (350 km) powerplant Mercedes D III output 160 hp (119.2 kW)
ARMAMENT:	two fixed Maxim LMG 08/15 7.92 mm machine guns immediately forward of the cockpit
FIRST FLIGHT DATE:	August 1916
OPERATORS:	Germany, Austria-Hungary, Turkey
PRODUCTION:	1532

Designed to wrest from the Allies the aerial superiority gained by the Nieuport 11 Bébé and Airco DH 2 over the once all-conquering Fokker E III, the Albatros-Werke machines made their combat debut in the summer of 1916. The first of the genus, the D I and D II had an immediate impact on the air war in the autumn of that year, these fighters establishing new standards in airframe elegance. Boasting a neatly-cowled Mercedes D III inline engine and a carefully streamlined semi-monocoque wooden fuselage, the Albatros scout looked like nothing else at the front at that time. They were also the first quantity-produced fighters to mount twin-synchronised machine guns. The D III was a further evolution of the Albatros D I/II design, this version abandoning the solid parallel-structure single-bay wing cellule in favour of the lighter, lower-drag Nieuport-style sesquiplane cellule. Some 400 were ordered by the Germans in October 1916, and production examples reached frontline *Jastas* from December of that same year. Early D IIIs suffered from chronic wing failure in the first months of operational service due to torsional flexibility of the lower wing – reinforced wings were introduced with the second batch of 840 machines. The D III was also licence-built by Oeffag in Austria, and these were progressively fitted with more powerful engines that produced up to 225 hp. Some 220 examples were also supplied to the Austro-Hungarians in 1917-18, and Poland procured 60 Oeffag-built machines post-war. The D III disappeared from service over the Western Front during mid 1918, but saw combat with the Austro-Hungarians until war's end.

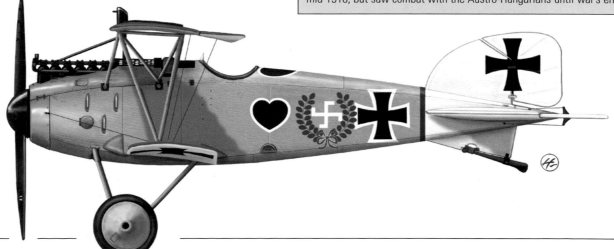

NUNGESSER'S NIEUPORT

'He succeeded in downing his adversary, which caught fire and exploded in front of the French trenches.'

A much bemedalled Charles Nungesser is seen wearing both French and foreign decorations, including the British Military Cross (*via Norman Franks*)

A true 'knight of the air' who preferred to be in the thick of the action rather than writing about it, French ace Charles Nungesser left few definitive accounts of his numerous exploits in combat over the Western Front. There was, however, the following official citation which accompanied the presentation of the *Legion d'Honneur* to Nungesser in early December 1915 after he had claimed his second aerial victory;

'Pilot detached at his own request to an *escadrille*. He has never ceased since his arrival to seek any occasion to fly, flying up to four hours and thirty minutes each day in spite of the inclement weather. During the course of the last combat he gave proof of the highest moral qualities by approaching to within ten metres of the enemy machine he was pursuing, firing in response up to the last moment. He succeeded in downing his adversary, which caught fire and exploded in front of the French trenches.'

A number of Nungesser's contemporaries committed their opinions of him to paper, including leading Belgian ace Willy Coppens, who wrote in his diary;

'A square-set figure of medium build, very fair-haired, with eyes as blue as cornflowers — deep luminous eyes, whose glance impressed themselves upon the memory. His whole person expressed indomitable energy, and in every way he was comparable to the heroes of medieval history whom we used to worship in our youth.'

A highly successful ace with 37 victories to his credit, Coppens was influenced by Nungesser in combat, as he related in his book *Days on the Wing*, published in 1934;

'A few days previously I had met Charles Nungesser, the wonderful French ace who was always getting wounded, but who always came up smiling after every fresh setback. Nungesser had propounded, in my hearing, this very sound argument — a two-seater aeroplane, when attacked over enemy territory by a single-seater possessed of greater speed, must accept the fight and turn sharply whenever the single-seater dives upon it. The single-seater, in effect, can only fire straight ahead, along its axis of flight. It follows that it cannot hold a two-seater for long in its sights, if the two-seater twists and turns, while the observer in the latter keeps the Scout under fire by means of his moveable gun. I remembered this piece of advice, and kept continuously turning — first one way and then the other, rarely coming back for more than a second onto an even keel.'

Coppens' memoir, which had originally been published in French as *Jours envolés*, was translated into English by RAF pilot A J Insall. The latter had also met Nungesser, and he added to *Days on the Wing;*

'The translator had the privilege of knowing this very excellent French pilot. Nungesser was a born fighter, with the eyes of a Norseman and the fire-eating "guts" of the Southerner. On one occasion, circa the spring of 1918, he broke out of hospital with his foot in plaster-of-Paris and returned to his squadron because he had heard that René Fonck, his greatest rival, had reached his

Nungesser's distinctively marked Nieuport 17bis N1895 parked in front of a Voisin VIII bomber of VB116. Note the broad bands across the top surfaces of the Nieuport's wings (*via Jon Guttman*)

own total of "*Victoires Homologuées*" (officially confirmed successes). France lost a great son when Charles Nungesser dared the might of the Atlantic.'

The distinguished British bomber pilot Charles P O Bartlett DSC wrote of his experiences in 5 Naval Squadron (later No 205 Sqn RAF) in his book *Bomber Pilot 1916-1918*, first published by Ian Allan in 1974. He included a few notes about Nungesser in his diaries;

'9 May 1917. After lunch, several of us went over to St Pol. We studied Nungesser's 130 hp Nieuport with his device of skull and crossbones, coffin and candlesticks enclosed in a large heart emblazoned on the side of his fuselage.

'28 May 1917. It transpires that Nungesser followed us over to Ghent and had a scrap with four enemy aircraft between Ghent and Bruges, one of them driving him down from 14,000 to 4000 ft, and making rings around his 160 hp Nieuport, which was badly shot about. He delights in lone expeditions.

'17 June 1917. I left at 0840 hrs for Bruges docks. On my way back, Nungesser came and stunted around me in his Nieuport off La Panne, his stripings and skull, crossbones, coffin and candlesticks showing up very vividly.'

Finally, an unnamed American pilot who served in the *Lafayette Escadrille* left the following account after meeting the oft-wounded Nungesser;

'Last night we had Nungesser here for dinner – a wonderful chap, blond and handsome, blue eyes, and rather square, clean-cut face, slightly sandy moustache. A striking feature is his smile, which reveals two solid rows of gold teeth. He has lost all his own teeth and wears a silver jaw. He also walks with a limp, his left leg being a little out of kilter.'

The third-ranking French fighter ace with 43 victories (almost 30 of which were scored on Nieuports), the incomparable Charles Nungesser of N65 was famed as much for his injuries as for his overall score – it was said that he had broken every major bone in his body at least once! He was also well known for his macabre personal insignia, which is clearly visible in this photograph of his then new Nieuport 17bis N1895, taken on 8 December 1916. Nungesser even went as far as to have a similar badge sewn onto his shirt pocket. After having been mistakenly attacked by a British fighter (and forced to shoot it down), he had broad red, white and blue bands applied to the upper wing and top fuselage decking of his aircraft in an effort to aid recognition. Nungesser's scouts also occasionally had these bands painted on the uppersurfaces of the lower wings as well (*via Jon Guttman*)

PILOT BIOGRAPHY – CHARLES NUNGESSER

Charles Eugene Jules Marie Nungesser was born in Paris on 15 March 1892. Dropping out of school, he travelled to Brazil to work in his uncle's sugar plantation, but ended up finding employment in Argentina as a car mechanic. He then started racing cars professionally in South America at the age of 17, where he met another Frenchman who had access to an aeroplane. Nungesser talked his friend into letting him take the Bleriot into the air by himself, and after flying it around for a few minutes, he made a successful landing. Within two weeks he had refined his flying abilities and started his career in aviation.

Returning to France following the outbreak of war, Nungesser joined the 2nd Hussars as a private. He requested, and was approved for, a transfer to the *Service Aeronautique* at around this time. Receiving his brevet on 2 March 1915, Nungesser was sent to VB106, then moved to N65, having achieved one victory in a Voisin two-seater. However, soon after arriving at his new unit he took off without permission, so although he received the *Croix de Guerre*, he was also placed under close arrest for eight days!

Gaining his second victory in December, Nungesser became a *Chevalier de la Légion d'Honneur*. Badly injured in a crash on 6 February 1916, which saw both of his legs broken, he returned to be commissioned, and in April began scoring victories. Wounded in combat on 19 May, he was back in action within a few days. By the end of 1916 Nungesser had claimed 21 victories, but had been injured again in June. He had also received the Military Cross from the British. In early 1917 Nungesser had to return to hospital because of his earlier injuries, but he managed to persuade his superiors not to ground him. Getting himself attached to V116, with his own Nieuport, he added nine more confirmed victories to his tally by August 1917.

In December Nungesser was injured yet again, this time in a car crash, but after treatment, and a month as an instructor, the ace returned to his old unit – now SPA65. Although the rest of the *escadrille* now flew SPADs, he still continued with later versions of the Nieuport adorned with his distinctive fuselage insignia of a black heart, as well as large red, white and blue stripes on the wings and top decking. In May 1918, with his score at 35, Nungesser was made an Officer of the *Légion d'Honneur*. By mid August he had claimed a total of 43 victories, plus 11 probables.

Post-war, Nungesser flew many crowd-pulling aerial shows, and then came the chance to fly the Atlantic with old friend Francois Coli. The pair took off on 8 May 1927 in a Levasseur PL 8 but were never seen again. At one stage it was said he had had every major bone in his body broken at least once, and he often flew before previous injuries had properly healed.

SPECIFICATION

Nieuport 17bis

TYPE:	single-seat, single-engined biplane fighter
ACCOMMODATION:	pilot
DIMENSIONS:	length 19 ft 0 in (5.80 m)
	wingspan 26 ft 9 in (8.16 m)
	height 7 ft 10 in (2.40 m)
WEIGHTS:	empty 825 lb (375 kg)
	maximum take-off 1263 lb (573 kg)
PERFORMANCE:	maximum speed 118 mph (190 kmh)
	range, endurance of 1.75 hours
	powerplant Clerget 9B
	output 130 hp (96.6 kW)
ARMAMENT:	one fixed 7.7 mm Vickers machine gun immediately forward of the cockpit and one moveable 7.7 mm Lewis gun over the top wing
FIRST FLIGHT DATE:	late 1916
OPERATORS:	France, UK
PRODUCTION:	less than 150

The highly successful Nieuport family of fighters were unique in their adoption of the sesquiplane wing layout, which saw them use the same wing design as a biplane, but with the lower wing possessing less than half the area of the upper flying surface. Supported by unique V-shaped interplane struts, the Nieuports were amongst the lightest and most manoeuvrable scouts of World War 1 thanks to the sesquiplane layout. Tracing its lineage directly back to the revolutionary Nieuport 11 Bébé of early 1916, the Nieuport 17 proved to be an outstanding success, despite suffering more than its fair share of wing shedding. The most successful of all sesquiplane fighters, the 17 equipped every French *escadrille de chasse* at some point during 1916. The standard 17 enjoyed almost a year of unparalleled success in combat, effectively ending the Fokker 'scourge'. In an effort to keep the machine competitive in combat, Nieuport produced the 17bis in late 1916, this version featuring a 130 hp Clerget 9B engine in place of the 110/120 hp Le Rhône 9Ja/Jb which had powered the standard 17. The aircraft also boasted full length fuselage side fairings. These modifications did very little to improve the scout's overall performance, however, and only a small number of 17bis were delivered to the French and the RNAS.

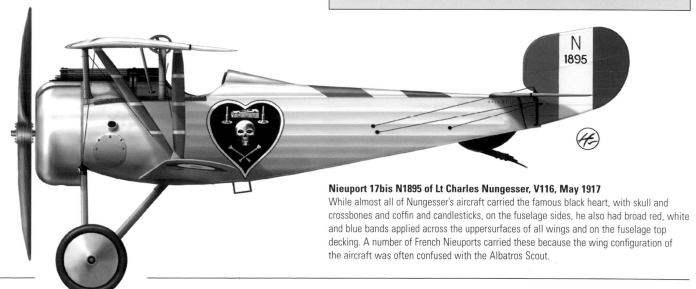

Nieuport 17bis N1895 of Lt Charles Nungesser, V116, May 1917
While almost all of Nungesser's aircraft carried the famous black heart, with skull and crossbones and coffin and candlesticks, on the fuselage sides, he also had broad red, white and blue bands applied across the uppersurfaces of all wings and on the fuselage top decking. A number of French Nieuports carried these because the wing configuration of the aircraft was often confused with the Albatros Scout.

FIGHTING 'COCKS'

'I managed to chase one and catch up with him. He was going down, weaving to avoid my bursts of fire, but I got his engine and he had to make an emergency landing in our lines.'

An official portrait of Capitaine Armand de Turenne, taken during his successful spell as CO of *Escadrille* SPA12 in 1918 (*via Jon Guttman*)

On 6 July 1917, Lts Armand de Turenne (in the SPAD VII seen in the foreground of the artwork opposite) and Georges Matton, CO of SPA48, were patrolling near Reims when they encountered six Albatros D Vs just over the French side of the frontline. Turenne eagerly attacked, but two of the German pilots quickly succeeded in getting on his tail. Coming to his aid, Matton managed to shoot one of the scouts down, and as the others fled back home, Turenne hit the engine of a second D V with a burst of fire. His victim was Vizefeldwebel Manfred Stimmel of *Jasta* 32, who force-landed between Courcy and Thil. Lt Matton attempted to land alongside the near-intact Albatros in an effort to prevent the pilot from sabotaging his machine, but the Frenchman's SPAD nosed over and he suffered minor injuries. Turenne later recalled;

'I was flying with my squadron leader Georges Matton, who would have become one of the greatest aces had he not been killed in action after his ninth victory. We were stationed near Rheims, and Matton asked me to go with him on a patrol over the lines. Before we got there, we met a group of six Albatros slightly on our side of the lines. Eager to show my squadron leader, I rushed onto them, took a shot at them and missed.

Immediately, I had two of them on my tail and was in a very bad spot. Matton chased one of the Germans and shot him down, then the others fled toward the German lines.

'I managed to chase one and catch up with him. He was going down, weaving to avoid my bursts of fire, but I got his engine and he had to make an emergency landing in our lines. I circled over him (Stimmel) because I could see his propeller still turning. Then I saw the pilot jump out of the machine and lay on the ground while the aeroplane rolled along and crashed into a fence 50 yards ahead. The German had sabotaged his machine according to orders.'

Vizefeldwebel Stimmel was quickly taken prisoner, and the two downed German fighters were jointly credited to both SPAD pilots. These D Vs were Matton's eighth and ninth victories, and Turenne's third and fourth of an eventual tally of fifteen.

As Turenne noted, his CO, Capitaine Jean Georges Fernand Matton, was destined to fall in combat when next he engaged German scouts. Having scored his first victory with N57 on

29 July 1916, Matton had been transferred to take command of N48 in early 1917, and while with this unit he had increased his score to nine, including the two enemy fighters on 6 July 1917. GC11, then comprising SPA12, SPA31, SPA48 and SPA57, accompanied GC12 to Flanders in late July, but there Matton, too, became a casualty of the intense fighting over that sector. He was killed in action on 10 September by Leutnant der Reserve Josef Jacobs, CO of *Jasta* 7. The latter, who would survive the war with a tally of more than 40 victories, was flying either an Albatros D V or a Pfalz D IIIa when he defeated Matton in combat.

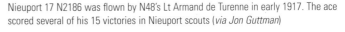
Nieuport 17 N2186 was flown by N48's Lt Armand de Turenne in early 1917. The ace scored several of his 15 victories in Nieuport scouts (*via Jon Guttman*)

Armand de Turenne poses alongside an Albatros D V that he and Capitaine J G F Matton shot down on 6 July 1917. The German aircraft, flown by Vizefeldwebel Manfred Stimmel of *Jasta* 32, crashed at 1150 hrs between Courcy and Thil, near Reims. Its pilot was taken prisoner (*via Jon Guttman*)

Capitaine de Turenne is seen with the SPAD XIII that he flew while serving as CO of *Escadrille* SPA12. He claimed nine of his fifteen kills while leading the unit (*via Jon Guttman*)

SPA48's Armand de Turenne stands beside his SPAD VII, which is decorated with the large cockerel's head emblem that he helped design for the *escadrille*. The future ace had joined N48 on 14 June 1916 (*via Jon Guttman*)

PILOT BIOGRAPHY – ARMAND DE TURENNE

Armand Jean Galliot Joseph de Turenne was born on 1 April 1891 in Le Mans, the son of a former infantry officer. Upon his graduation from school, he enlisted for three years military duty with 10éme *Regiment de Chasseurs* in April 1909. Following a brief return to civilian life, Turenne re-enlisted in the 21ére *Regiment de Dragoons* in February 1913. Promoted to officer candidate in August of the following year, he requested a transfer to the aviation service in July 1915 and received his brevet as a pilot on 21 December that same year following the completion of his training at Pau.

Turenne was posted to Nieuport-equipped *Escadrille* N48 (led by Lt Georges Matton) on 14 June 1916, and after seeing much action over the Verdun front, he scored his first victory on 17 November when he downed an Albatros. By the end of September 1917 he had increased his tally to six victories (all fighting scouts), and his leadership qualities were recognised on 12 January the following year when he was made CO of *Escadrille* SPA12. Under Turenne's leadership, the unit was cited in General Orders on 14 May 1918 for having downed 34 aircraft and two balloons.

Promoted to capitaine in July 1918, Turenne claimed his last two victories on 26 September in an action which almost cost him his life. Wounded twice already during the course of the year while attacking observation balloons, he destroyed another near Verdun for his 14th victory, but was then set upon by several Fokker D VIIs. Turenne's SPAD XIII was badly shot up and the Frenchman slightly wounded, but by playing dead he managed to lure one of his attackers into an advantageous position and shoot him down for his final victory. During the final month of the war Turenne was placed in command of *Groupe de Combat* 11.

Remaining in military service post-war, Turenne had made full colonel by March 1937. He again fought for his country in 1939-40 as commander of *Groupe de Chasse* 24, and was promoted to a Grand Officier de la Legion d'Honneur on 25 December 1941. Turenne finally passed away in December 1980.

SPAD VII (serial unknown) of Lt Armand de Turenne, SPA48, July 1917
Turenne claimed that he and his commander, Lt Georges Matton, co-designed the cockerel's head within a blue halo that was ultimately adopted as N48's squadron insignia, along with the motto '*Chant et Combat*' ('Crow and Fight'). In addition to the cockerel insignia and the number '2', Turenne retained the family coat of arms that had graced the side of his earlier Nieuport 11, applied under the cockpit of his SPAD VII. Later, when he took command of SPA12 in 1918, Turenne retained the SPA 48 cockerel's head as a personal marking in place of SPA12's usual blue and white pennant, but dispensed with an individual numeral, since his marking was unique within the *escadrille*.

SPECIFICATION

SPAD VII

TYPE: single-seat, single-engined biplane fighter

ACCOMMODATION: pilot

DIMENSIONS: length 19 ft 11.3 in (6.08 m)
wingspan 25 ft 8 in (7.82 m)
height 7 ft 2.75 in (2.20 m)

WEIGHTS: empty 1102 lb (500 kg)
maximum take-off 1552 lb (704 kg)

PERFORMANCE: maximum speed 132 mph (212 kmh)
range, endurance of 1.85 hours
powerplant Hispano-Suiza HS 8Ab
output 180 hp (134 kW)

ARMAMENT: One fixed Vickers 7.7 mm machine gun immediately forward of the cockpit

FIRST FLIGHT DATE: April 1916

OPERATORS: France, UK, USA, Russia, Belgium, Italy

PRODUCTION: 5500

The end result of the design trend of 1915-16 which saw heavier, more powerful and less agile fighting scouts appearing from the warring nations of Europe, the SPAD VII was easily the most successful aircraft of this period to emerge from France. Powered by the superb, but often temperamental, Hispano-Suiza V8 engine, the 150 hp SPAD VII prototype had flown for the first time in April 1917. The aircraft had an impressive top speed in both level flight and in the dive, but lacked the manoeuvrability of contemporary Nieuports. However, combat reports received from the front had suggested that pilots valued high speed over agility, hence the heavy fighter route chosen by SPAD. Production examples began reaching French combat units in the summer of 1916, but the delivery tempo was slow due to production difficulties with the scout's V8 engine. The SPAD VII entered combat with both the French *Aviation Militaire* and the RFC at much the same time, and once its engine maladies had been rectified, the fighter enjoyed great success over the Western Front. Most French *escadrille de chasse* flew the SPAD VII at some stage in World War 1, and the aircraft also saw action with Belgian, Italian, American and Russian units during the conflict.

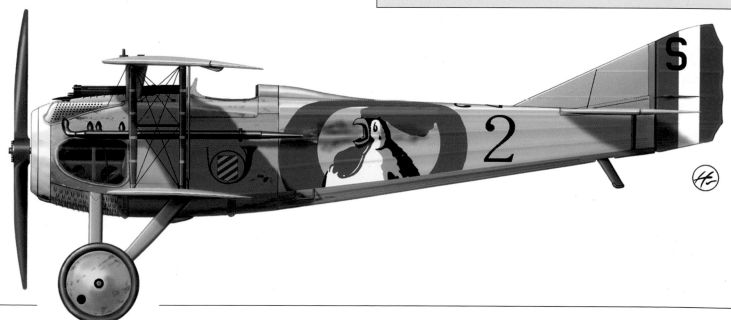

'NAVAL 10' ACE

'About eight enemy aircraft dived on us and about 20 more attacked on our level. There was a general dogfight.'

Flt Sub-Lt Lawrence Coombes DFC scored 15 victories with 10 Naval Squadron/No 210 Sqn between March and July 1918 (*via Norman Franks*)

The Sopwith Camels of the RNAS's 10 Naval Squadron were amongst the most colourful British fighting scouts to see action over the Western Front in World War 1. This Iain Wyllie artwork features Camel B6358, which was the regular mount of the unit's second-ranking ace Flt Sub-Lt Lawrence P Coombes, who claimed 15 kills with 'Naval 10'. The aircraft is seen here when in service with the RNAS unit in the spring of 1918, flying from Treizennes, in northern France. Its blue and white horizontal stripes and wheel covers, as well as the letter 'C', reveal its assignment to the unit's 'C' Flight – 'A' Flight used black and white stripes and 'B' Flight red and white. The white vertical stripes on the aircraft's fuselage were exclusively used by 'Naval 10' after August 1917. Finally, the wheel cover designs varied from fighter to fighter, but they were always in flight colours.

A long-lived Camel, B6358 was flown by Coombes from February through to June 1918, during which time the unit (along with the rest of the RNAS) reverted to RFC control and was redesignated No 210 Sqn.

In the spring of 1918, soon after the creation of the Royal Air Force on 1 April, Coombes and No 210 Sqn saw much action attacking enemy targets on the ground in an attempt to blunt the Germans' latest push in the bitterly contested Ypres sector. He recalled;

'The Germans began another big offensive early in April, near Ypres, which was close to where we were based. The Portuguese held the line near Ypres, and they gave up when the Germans attacked, retreating in disorder. A big salient formed at this point

Colourful Camels of 10 Naval Squadron sit side-by-side at Teteghem, near Dunkirk, in early 1918. B6299 in the foreground was flown by eight-victory ace Flt Lt N M MacGregor, who served with the unit's 'B' Flight in 1917-18 (*via Norman Franks*)

of weakness, and the front was in such a state of flux that nobody knew where it was, and one had to be careful to distinguish friend from foe when ground strafing.

'The weather was bad around 8 April – low cloud and mist – so we were sent to ground strafe and drop 20-lb bombs on any targets we could find.

'On 11 April I was on another low bombing patrol. After dropping bombs on some barges and firing at transport vehicles, I was flying at 300 ft when I was shot up from the ground. The engine stopped and I prepared to force-land when I felt petrol soaking the seat of my pants. I realised that the main pressure tank on which the pilot sat was holed, so I switched to the gravity tank and the engine picked up. When I got back, it was found that besides the petrol tank, two cylinders had been pierced – it was a miracle the engine kept going.'

Ground strafing often provoked a response from German *Jastas* in the area, as was the case on 11 May 1918 in the action depicted in this artwork. Lawrence Coombes remembered;

'A patrol of 24 British and Australian Camels did a high offensive patrol on this date. We dropped 92 bombs on Armentières and set fire to an ammunition dump. About eight enemy aircraft dived on us, and about 20 more attacked on our level. There was a general dogfight, one Australian Camel going down in flames while Alexander (23-victory ace Flt Lt William Melville Alexander) of 210 got an enemy aircraft also in flames. I shot down an Albatros out of control.

'Turning for home, we discovered that a ground mist had suddenly come up, covering a huge area of France. Nine of our squadron crashed – including myself – trying to land in fields, one being killed and one severely injured. Quite a number of Allied aircraft were taken by surprise and suffered similar fates.'

Flt Sub-Lt Lawrence Coombes leans on the lower wing of his Camel (B6358) at Teteghem in March 1918 (*via Norman Franks*)

PILOT BIOGRAPHY – LAWRENCE P COOMBES

Lawrence Percival Coombes was born in India on 9 April 1899, and he was just 19 when he joined the RNAS in June 1917. Upon completion of his pilot training he was posted to Teteghem-based 10 Naval Squadron, via 'Naval 12', in late January 1918. Coombes made his first claim just before his outfit became No 210 Sqn RAF, and by the end of July he had increased his score to 15 victories, and been awarded the DFC for his successes in combat.

One of the Camel ace's more memorable sorties occurred on 26 June when he and fellow aces Ivan Sanderson and American Ken Unger accounted for four Fokker D VIIs. One of the latter was flown by 13-kill Marine ace Kurt Schönfelder of *Jasta* 7, who had shot down Camel ace Pruett M Dennett of No 208 Sqn on 2 June (the German's last victory, claimed on 21 June, had also been a No 210 Sqn Camel).

Post-war, Coombes became a barnstormer, before completing an engineering degree and finding employment with the Royal Aeronautical Establishment at Farnborough. He then moved to the Marine Aircraft Experimental Establishment at Felixstowe, and in 1927 was part of the Schneider Trophy team during the Venice races. In 1938 Coombes emigrated to Australia, where he worked for the federal government in aeronautical research. He was seconded to the United Nations in 1960, and eventually became chairman of the Commonwealth Advisory Aeronautical Research Council and chief supervisor at the Aeronautical Research Labs. Coombes passed away in Melbourne, Australia, on 2 June 1988.

SPECIFICATION

Sopwith Camel

TYPE:	single-seat, single-engined biplane fighter
ACCOMMODATION:	one pilot
DIMENSIONS:	length 18 ft 9 in (5.72 m) wingspan 28 ft 0 in (8.53 m) height 8 ft 6 in (2.59 m)
WEIGHTS:	empty 929 lb (421 kg) maximum take-off 1453 lb (659 kg)
PERFORMANCE:	maximum speed 113 mph (182 kmh) range, endurance of 2.5 hours powerplant Clerget 9B, Bentley BR1 or Le Rhône output 130 hp (96.6 kW)
ARMAMENT:	two fixed Vickers 0.303-in machine guns immediately forward of the cockpit, and optional underwing racks for four 25 lb (11.3 kg) bombs
FIRST FLIGHT DATE:	22 December 1916
OPERATORS:	UK, USA
PRODUCTION:	5490

The most famous British fighter of World War 1, the Camel was also the most successful design to see service with either side in respect to the number of victories – 1294 aeroplanes and three airships – claimed by the men who flew it. Designed by Herbert Smith, the Camel was the first purpose-built fighting scout to boast two Vickers machine guns synchronised to fire through the propeller arc. The humped fairing covering the breeches of these weapons actually provided the inspiration for the fighter's unique sobriquet which, like its predecessor the Pup, went from being an unofficial appellation to its official name. Although the Camel boasted a fearsome reputation in combat, the fighter's exacting handling characteristics took a heavy toll on poorly trained novice pilots. Nevertheless, almost 5500 Camels were eventually built, with the Sopwith design seeing service on the Western Front with British (and American) units from May 1917 until war's end. It was also flown by Home Defence units in England on nightfighter patrols, and saw action on the Italian front with RFC/RAF squadrons. Finally, land-based RNAS squadrons saw considerable action along the North Sea coast with early examples of the Camel, before being amalgamated into the newly-formed RAF on 1 April 1918.

Camel B6358 of Flt Sub-Lt Lawrence P Coombes, 10 Naval Squadron, Treizennes, France, spring 1918

Coombes used B6358 to gain his first two victories. The aircraft had previously been on the strength of the Seaplane Defence Flight, where Flt Sub-Lt J E Greene had destroyed a balloon with it and had then endured a minor force landing on 4 December 1917. Going to 9 Naval Squadron, the Camel had been used by Flt Sub-Lt M S Taylor to drive down a DFW in January, and after its spell with 10 Naval Squadron, B6358 went to No 213 Sqn. Here, Lt G D Smith shared a victory while flying the aircraft on 7 July. The veteran fighting scout was lost on 25 August 1918. While a part of 10 Naval Squadron, the Camel featured the unit's blue and white stripes, reaching back to the cockpit.

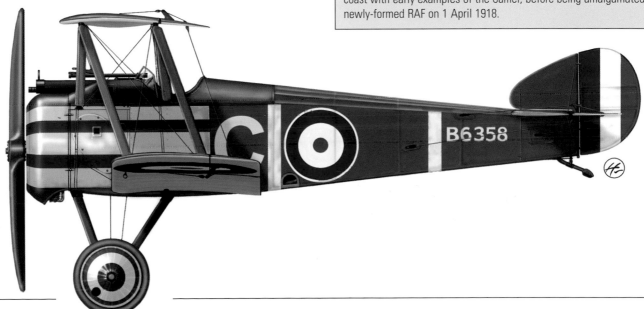

THE 'RED KNIGHT'

'I put myself behind the adversary and brought him down, burning, with only a few shots.'

On 20 April 1918 Rittmeister Manfred Freiherr von Richthofen, commander of *Jagdgeschwader* Nr I, achieved his 79th and 80th victories to become the 'ace of aces' of all nations in World War 1. Led by Richthofen in his scarlet Fokker Dr I 425/17, seven Triplanes of *Jagdstaffel* 11 had engaged a patrol of Camels from No 3 Sqn of the newly-formed RAF east of Villers-Brettoneaux. Seeing a Fokker being attacked by one of the British fighters, the Rittmeister fastened onto the tail of the Camel, flown by Maj Richard Raymond-Barker. After only a few accurate shots from Richthofen's guns, the Camel (D6439) exploded in flames and Raymond-Barker was killed.

With scarcely a pause, Richthofen was soon firing at Camel B7393, flown by 19-year-old Rhodesian 2Lt David G Lewis. The fighter's fuel tanks were hit and set on fire, but Lewis managed to cut his engine and dive to the ground, being thrown clear from the crash. Dazed, scorched, but alive, Lewis staggered to his feet and saw the blazing wreckage of Raymond-Barker's machine only 50 yards away. Richthofen soared overhead at low level and waved at German infantry who were coming to take Lewis prisoner. The young Rhodesian pilot subsequently wrote the following account of his encounter with the 'Red Knight' on this day;

'On the evening of 20 April, 12 of us left the aerodrome on an offensive patrol led by Capt Douglas Bell of my flight ('C' Flight), although the CO, Maj Raymond-Barker, was with us. The day had been a stormy one, with intermittent squalls, and there were still heavy clouds in the sky when we reached the German lines.

'Knowing that the German anti-aircraft guns would have the range of the clouds, Bell thought it advisable to rise above them. In carrying this out, we lost touch in the clouds with the other flight, and continued the patrol six-strong.

'About four miles over the German lines, we met approximately fifteen German triplanes, which endeavoured to attack us from behind, but Bell frustrated this attempt by turning to meet them, so the fight started with the two patrols firing at each other head on. When the Germans came closer, we knew we had met Richthofen's circus – the machines of his squadron were always brilliantly coloured.

'A few seconds after the fight began, Maj Barker's petrol tank was hit by an incendiary bullet, which caused the tank to explode and shatter his machine. Bits of his machine were still reaching the ground when I was shot down.

'I was attacking a bright blue machine, which was level with me, and was about to finish this adversary off when I heard the rat-tat-tat of machine guns coming from behind me and saw the splintering of struts just above my head. I left my man and wheeled quickly to find that I was face to face with the renowned Richthofen – the baron always flew a bright red machine, that is how I knew it was he.

Rittmeister Manfred von Richthofen poses for an official photograph in early 1918. This image was turned into a postcard which was widely sold throughout Germany prior to the end of the war (*via Greg VanWyngarden*)

'I twisted and turned in the endeavour to avoid his line of fire, but he was too experienced a fighter, and only once did I manage to have him at a disadvantage, and then only for a few seconds, but in those few ticks of a clock I shot a number of bullets into his machine and thought I would have the honour of bringing him down, but in a trice the positions were reversed and he had set my emergency petrol tank alight, and I was hurtling earthward in flames.

'I hit the ground about four miles northeast of Villers-Bretonneaux at a speed of 60 mph, was thrown clear of my machine and except for minor burns, was unhurt.

Rittmeister Manfred von Richthofen sits on the wheel of a Fokker triplane which appears to be painted in factory finish – except perhaps for a red cowling? Note the manufacturer's plate on the cowling. Dogs were a favourite of many pilots, and here the Baron gazes at his Danish hound 'Moritz' (*via Greg VanWyngarden*)

'About 50 yards from where I was, Maj Barker's machine was burning fiercely, so I staggered over to the wreckage of his machine to see if it were possible to pull him out, but was beaten back by the flames.

'From the seat to the tail of my aeroplane, there was not a stitch of fabric left, it having been burned away. The following articles were hit by Richthofen's bullets; the compass, which was directly in front of my face, my goggles where the elastic joined the frame of the glass – these went over the side – the elbow of my coat, and one bullet through the leg of my trousers.

'The rest of my flight was saved from annihilation by the timely arrival of a squadron of SE 5as. Richthofen came down to within 100 ft of the ground and waved to me.'

Lewis was Richthofen's 80th, and final, victim. He was mistaken in his belief that the Rittmeister was waving at him, as the latter pilot's combat report reveals. He believed that his final opponent was quite dead, so he must have been waving at the triumphant German infantry who had appeared to take Lewis prisoner. Richthofen's combat report of the same incident read as follows;

'With six aeroplanes of *Staffel* 11, I attacked a large enemy squadron. During the fight, I observed that a triplane was attacked and shot down from below by a Camel. I put myself behind the adversary and brought him down, burning, with only a few shots. The enemy aircraft dashed down near the forest of Hamel, where it burned further on the ground.

'Three minutes after I had brought down the first machine I attacked a second Camel of the same enemy squadron. The adversary dived, caught his machine and repeated this manoeuvre several times. I approached him as near as possible when fighting, and fired 50 bullets until the machine began to burn. The body of the machine was burned in the air, the remnants dashed to the ground northeast of Villers-Bretonneux.'

Richthofen's final Dr I was 425/17, which is seen here at Léchelle in late March 1918 – prior to having its cross markings modified. Note the cover over the fighter's propeller. This was the aircraft in which the 'Red Knight' was shot down and killed on 21 April 1918 (*via Greg VanWyngarden*)

PILOT BIOGRAPHY – MANFRED VON RICHTHOFEN

The most successful fighter pilot of World War 1 was born on 2 May 1892 in the Lower Silesian town of Kleinberg, near Schweidnitz. His father was a retired career Army officer, and Manfred was destined to follow in his footsteps – he entered the Cadet Institute at Wahlstatt at the age of 11. He graduated to the Main Cadet Institute at Gross-Lichterfelde in 1909, and was commissioned as a leutnant in the Silesian Ulanen-Regiment (Kaiser Alexander III von Russland) Nr 1 in 1912. When the war began Richthofen's unit was sent to the eastern front, and he saw service both in Russia and then France. Dissatisfied with the inaction he experienced on the latter front, he petitioned to transfer to the air service, which he did in May 1915.

After training as an observer, Richthofen was sent back to the eastern front with *Fledflieger Abteilung* 69, then served with *Brieftauben Abteilung Ostende* (BAO) – a cover name for a multi-task unit which operated over the Flanders Front. After a chance meeting with leading ace Oswald Boelcke, he was inspired to pursue pilot training, and completed this in December 1915. While serving as a pilot with *Kampfgeschwader* 2 in Russia, Richthofen was recruited for Boelcke's new *Jasta* 2. Flying the Albatros D II, he rewarded Boelcke's faith in him by downing an FE 2b on 17 September 1916 – the momentous first of an eventual 80 victories. After Boelcke's death on 28 October, Richthofen really showed his promise when he downed the DH 2 of Maj Lanoe G Hawker, the CO of No 24 Sqn and Britain's premier fighter tactician, on 23 November for his 11th victory.

On 10 January 1917 he was made commander of *Jasta* 11, and two days later received the news of his *Pour le Mérite*, which followed his 24th claim. As a *Staffelführer*, Richthofen proved to be as skilful a leader, trainer and organiser as he was a fighter pilot. He rose to the rank of *Rittmeister* on 6 April.

By the end of 'Bloody April' Richthofen had surpassed his idol Boelcke's score with 53 victories, and his *Jasta* 11 was famous throughout Germany. It was only logical that he be given command of the first Fighter Wing in the *Luftstreitkräfte*, but his leadership of *Jagdgeschwader* Nr I was soon interrupted by a near-fatal head wound of 6 July.

Richthofen returned to combat far too soon, plagued by headaches and exhaustion after every flight. Nonetheless, his was a war of duty, and he persevered. Although many of his superiors and family urged him to retire from combat flying, he refused. In March and April 1918 he seemed to be back to his old form, scoring 16 kills in less than six weeks. His death on 21 April remains a subject of controversy, but his score would not be surpassed in World War 1, nor would his legend.

SPECIFICATION

Fokker Dr I

TYPE:	single-seat, single-engined triplane fighter
ACCOMMODATION:	one pilot
DIMENSIONS:	length 18 ft 11 in (5.77 m) wingspan 23 ft 7.5 in (7.17 m) height 9 ft 8 in (2.95 m)
WEIGHTS:	empty 904 lb (410 kg) maximum take-off 1289 lb (585 kg)
PERFORMANCE:	maximum speed 103 mph (165 kmh) range, endurance of 1.5 hours powerplant Obursel Ur II output 110 hp (96.6 kW)
ARMAMENT:	two fixed Maxim LMG 08/15 7.92 mm machine guns immediately forward of the cockpit
FIRST FLIGHT DATE:	June 1917
OPERATOR:	Germany
PRODUCTION:	320

Although aeronautical designers in Germany had been experimenting with triplane designs from aviation's earliest days, it was the appearance of the RNAS's Sopwith Triplane over the Western Front in late 1916 that prompted the hasty development of the Dr I. Created by Fokker's design team, the Dr I was a compact fighting scout that boasted wings without 'bracing' – it had no flying, landing or incidence wires, the airframe's strength instead coming from an original single-spar arrangement which was actually two boxspars joined vertically. Following successful type testing, the Dr I was ordered into production on 14 July 1917. The soundness of the design was proven the following month when two pre-production prototypes were tested at the front by Richthofen and fellow ace Werner Voss. An incredibly manoeuvrable aircraft about all axes, and very tiring to fly, the Dr I proved formidable with a skilled aviator at the controls, despite being rather slow and restricted to combat at lower altitudes. Briefly grounded in November 1917 due to a spate of wing failures caused by poor workmanship, the aircraft had all but disappeared at the front by August 1918.

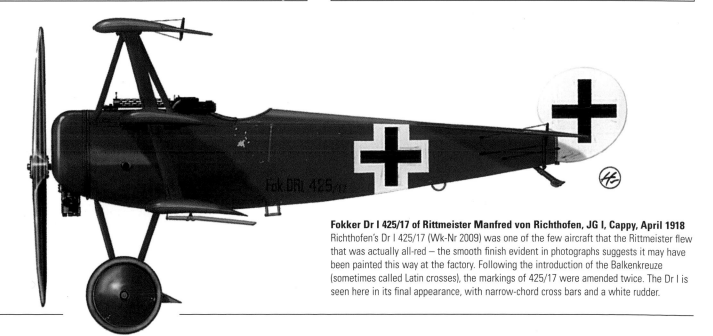

Fokker Dr I 425/17 of Rittmeister Manfred von Richthofen, JG I, Cappy, April 1918
Richthofen's Dr I 425/17 (Wk-Nr 2009) was one of the few aircraft that the Rittmeister flew that was actually all-red – the smooth finish evident in photographs suggests it may have been painted this way at the factory. Following the introduction of the Balkenkreuze (sometimes called Latin crosses), the markings of 425/17 were amended twice. The Dr I is seen here in its final appearance, with narrow-chord cross bars and a white rudder.

FIRST VICTORY

'Like a steer unbound, the aircraft with the Braunschweig Hussar's crest dived onto the enemy first.'

Georg von Hantelmann of *Jasta* 15 left us no first-hand accounts, save for a very terse combat report for his final victory, but we do have the account of his *Staffel* mate Joachim von Ziegesar, who was quite a writer. Von Ziegesar wrote the following in May 1933 for a memorial volume that von Hantelmann's sister was writing about her late brother.

He describes the action of 6 June 1918, when *Jasta* 15 attacked a flight of seven DH 4 bombers, probably from the RAF's No 27 Sqn, near Chaulnes. He erred in recalling their opponents as 'Frenchmen', a common enough mistake (aircraft identification was abysmal on both sides in World War 1). No 27 Sqn did lose DH 4 B2080, with its crew of Lt M F Cunningham and Lt W J Stockins both killed (probably by von Hantelmann). The squadron had two more DH 4's badly shot up, returning with wounded

For some reason, photographs of Ltn d R Georg von Hantelmann are scarce. One of the best shows the youthful ace posing for the cameraman in typical JG II fashion to mark his 20th victory, this shot being taken on 9 October 1918 at Charmois aerodrome. The Fokker's nose is decorated with a floral wreath to commemorate the occasion. On 4 November 1918, Hantelmann claimed his final victory in D VII 465/18, but it is not known if this is indeed that aircraft (*via Greg VanWyngarden*)

Fokkers D VIIs of JG II are seen scattered around the aerodrome at Chéry-les-Pouilly in August 1918. In the foreground is the arrow-decorated D VII of Hantelmann's *Jasta* commander, Josef Veltjens. In the middle distance is a line of white-nosed Fokkers of *Jasta* 12, and behind them can be seen *Jasta* 13 machines (*via Greg VanWyngarden*)

observers, but it was not annihilated as von Ziegesar claims. Von Hantelmann was probably flying his Fokker D VII 382/18, emblazoned with his personal insignia from his former cavalry unit, the Braunschweiger 'Death's Head' Hussar Regiment Nr 17. Here is von Ziegesar's account;

'I don't know how I could better begin memories of our good friend Georg von Hantelmann than with the story of 6 June 1918, when he conquered his first opponent in the air.

'The time of the Hindenburg Offensive lay behind us. The wild turbulent life of the war of movement had again turned into the monotony of the war of position. *Jagdstaffel* 15, which we belonged to, was the commander's *Staffel* of *Jagdgeschwader* 2, and was led by our unsurpassable Hauptmann Berthold. Because he had been seriously wounded in Flanders by an English explosive bullet, he could not yet fly, so that his replacement Leutnant (Josef) Veltjens – called "Seppl" by us – led the *Staffel* in the air. Besides this, these men belonged to our "club" at that time: Oberleutnant Turck, Leutnant von Buttlar, Leutnant von Beaulieu-Marconnay, Leutnant Schäfer, Leutnant Klein and the Vizefeldwebels Weischer and Klaudat, as well as myself.

'On 6 June we were situated on a small, wretched airfield right near the village of Mesnil, not far from the Somme. 6 June awakened us with radiating sunshine. According to orders, we made our flight to the Front early in the morning, without experiencing anything of consequence. Upon landing, the mechanics made our aircraft ready again, and we leisurely went to tents to prepare ourselves for a second take-off at ten o'clock.

'We were still standing around the airfield and talking when suddenly the report arrived from our radio position that an enemy squadron of seven aircraft from the hinterlands was nearing our area. With inimitable speed, we were dressed and sitting in our aircraft. Before every flight, the engine was first "braked" – a

hellish noise – then the aeroplanes were rolling up to take off. Veltjens, as leader, raised his hand and the wild chase was on. After a few minutes the *Staffel* was in its usual order. While we climbed with full running engines, "Seppl" led us to the Front so that we cut off the Frenchmen's (sic) way back. Soon, we were at 4000 metres – then we caught sight of them.

'The second bulge in our Front near Montdidier was good for them, and they attempted to escape to the south after they had also discovered us. In vain! Our aircraft were fast and our wills like iron to get the "cockades". Minutes passed – they seemed like an eternity to us. Now it was our turn. Veltjens stopped for a second, and then gave the sign to attack!

'Like a steer unbound, the aircraft with the Braunschweig Hussar's crest dived onto the enemy first. Even before we others had a chance to shoot, Hantelmann went down with his left wingman on the Frenchmen (sic) flying in arrow formation. For us, there wasn't any more time left to watch. Each one grabbed hold of his opponent and – as was normal in air fighting – only a few minutes passed by and the French (sic) squadron that was in the process of returning home, certainly with valuable reports and photographs, no longer existed!

'Radiating joy, we gathered together again around our leader and tried, flushed with victory, to find new battles, yet no opportunities offered themselves till the petrol has been used up by flying and we had to return to our airfield.

'We had hardly climbed out of our machines when the usual dispute arose. Everyone had to tell his story – it was determined, though, that Hantelmann was the first one to bag his opponent.

'It was not usual for us to throw big victory parties, but the *Staffel* received praise from Berthold, and we also bought ourselves a bottle of wine in the evening.'

On 17 June 1918, Ltn Georg von Hantelmann's *Jasta* 15 D VII was borrowed by new arrival Kurt Wüsthoff, a 27-victory ace from *Jasta* 4, for a fateful patrol. The flight of JG II aircraft engaged 15 SE 5as from No 24 Sqn, and Wüsthoff was brought down with a serious groin wound, landing the D VII behind French lines to become a prisoner. The fighter was turned over to the British, who gave it the number G/5/17 Bde. The D VII duly became the subject of great study (*via Greg VanWyngarden*)

PILOT BIOGRAPHY – GEORG VON HANTELMANN

Georg von Hantelmann was born on 9 October 1898. He joined the military in 1916, and on 15 June was commissioned into the Braunschweiger Hussar Regiment Nr 17 – the 'Death's Head Hussars' (the Death's Head insignia would decorate his Fokker). However, he soon transferred into the air service, and following his training he was sent to *Jasta* 18 on 6 February 1918, aged just 19. Swapping to *Jasta* 15, Hantelmann recorded his first success (a British DH 4 bomber) on 6 June, and by the end of that month his tally stood at four victories confirmed and three unconfirmed.

Issued with a Fokker D VII in July 1918, Hantelmann's score then began to rapidly increase. Two victories came in August, then 12 during September, including three on the 14th against the Americans. Seven more followed in October, and his 25th, and final, victory claim on 4 November almost got him the 'Blue Max', but the Kaiser's abdication saw him miss out.

Hantelmann's prowess in aerial combat is shown by some of the important Allied airmen he brought down. On 12 September 1918 he shot down Lt David Putnam, a 13-victory ace (with many probables) flying with the US 139th Aero Squadron – Putnam was two months younger than his German adversary, but he had already more than proved himself in action with both the French and the American air forces. On the 16th *Jasta* 15 attacked two SPADs that had just flamed a balloon, and Hantelmann brought down the one flown by the French ace Sous-Lt Maurice Boyau of SPA77, who had moments before attained his 35th victory. On the 18th he downed Joseph Wehner, the six-kill wingman and friend of Frank Luke Jr, who flew with the 27th Aero Squadron.

Surviving the war at just a month past his 20th birthday, Hantelmann was fated to die at the hands of Polish poachers on his estates in East Prussia on 7 September 1924.

SPECIFICATION
Fokker D VII

TYPE: single-seat, single-engined biplane fighter

ACCOMMODATION: one pilot

DIMENSIONS: length 22 ft 9.66 in (6.95 m)
wingspan 29 ft 2.333 in (8.90 m)
height 9 ft 0 in (2.75 m)

WEIGHTS: empty 1508 lb (684 kg)
maximum take-off 2006 lb (910 kg)

PERFORMANCE: maximum speed 116 mph (187 kmh)
range, endurance of 1.5 hours
powerplant Mercedes D IIIaü
output 180 hp (134 kW)

ARMAMENT: two fixed Maxim LMG 08/15 7.92 mm machine guns immediately forward of the cockpit

FIRST FLIGHT DATE: December 1917

OPERATOR: Germany

PRODUCTION: 2000+

Created by Fokker's highly talented design team, the prototype D VII was completed in great haste in late 1917 so that it could enter the German D-Type standard fighter competition held at Adlershof in January/February 1918. Emerging the clear winner, the D VII design boasted a simple, yet strong, welded-steel tube fuselage and cantilever wing cellule. It was put into widespread production by Fokker, as well as licensees Albatros and its subsidiary OAW. Once committed to frontline service with *Jagdgeschwader* I in May 1918, the D VII proved to be the best fighting scout in service with either side. Indeed, it was claimed that the Fokker could make a good pilot into an ace, and it set the standards against which all new fighters were measured for over a decade. Precise production figures for the D VII have been lost, but it is thought that somewhere in the region of 3200 were ordered and 2000+ delivered before the Armistice. Proof of the fighter's formidable reputation came when the victorious Allies specifically stated in the surrender terms dictated to Germany that all surviving D VIIs had to be handed over.

Fokker D VII 382/18 of Ltn Georg von Hantelmann, *Jasta* 15, Le Mesnil, June 1918
Hantelmann's D VII was being flown by new *Jasta* 15 member Ltn Kurt Wüsthoff when he was shot down and captured on 17 June 1918, and thus it became the subject of close scrutiny by the Allies. An early Fokker-built D VII, it left the factory with five-colour fabric on its wings and a streaked fuselage. At *Staffel* 15 it was given a red nose and wheels and a dark blue fuselage and tail, but the struts remained grey. The fuselage cross was still slightly visible beneath the blue paint. Hantelmann's skull and crossbones emblem was inspired by his former service as a 'death's head' hussar.

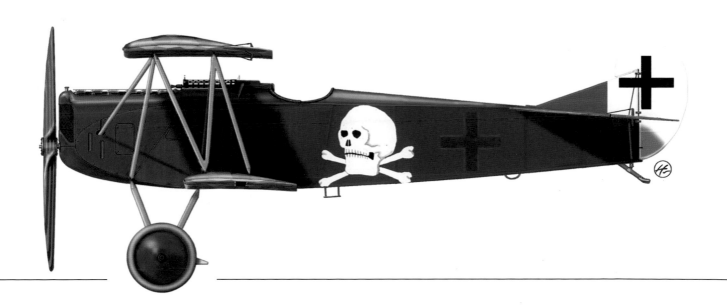

DUEL OVER THE DOLOMITES

'I turned towards him and we came head-on. He opened fire first, and a second later I replied.'

Frank Linke-Crawford poses in front of a Brandenburg D I of *Flik* 12. This particular aeroplane (65.54) crashed on 7 November 1916 with Oberst Emil Uzelac, commander of the *kaiserliche und königliche Luftfahrtruppen* (LFT), at the controls (*via Norman Franks*)

In early July 1918, the fourth ranking Austro-Hungarian ace Frank Linke-Crawford fought an inconclusive dogfight with a Sopwith Camel – almost certainly of the RAF's No 45 Sqn – on the southern edge of the Dolomites near Feltre. Both aircraft were damaged (Linke-Crawford flying Oberleutnant Jansky's Phönix D I at the time), although neither crashed. A month earlier, on 1 June, Linke-Crawford had emerged victorious in a similar dogfight with another Camel, as No 45 Sqn pilot Procter Huins recalled;

'We flew an early morning patrol over the lines, Earl Hand, Paddy O'Neill and myself. When seven to ten miles over the lines, at a height of 12,000 ft, a sudden waggling of wings by Hand told me that he had spotted some enemy aircraft well below us at 3000 ft. Down he went in a good dive, and I followed on, flattening out after the dive. Hand immediately closed in combat with a black machine with a large camouflaged letter "L" on the top centre section of the Albatros D V.

'I was about 100 yards away, and as I hurried on a parallel course, Hand turned out of the tight circle in which he and the enemy aircraft were involved, and I saw flames come from his main tank behind his back. The pilot of "L" was then about 100 yards away. I turned towards him and we came head-on. He opened fire first, and a second later I replied. After a burst of about two seconds, both of my guns jammed. I held my head-on approach and

Ranking Austro-Hungarian ace with 35 victories, Godwin Brumowski (left) and Frank Linke-Crawford discuss tactics in front of their Oeffag-built Albatros D IIIs in December 1917. Both men were serving with *Flik* 41J at the time (*via Norman Franks*)

Mechanics from *Flik* 41J briefly stop work for a group photograph soon after righting Frank Linke-Crawford's Oeffag-built Albatros D III 153.04 at Sesana in the late summer of 1917 (*via Norman Franks*)

decided to fly for a collision. At the last moment, when it seemed certain we would collide, the enemy aircraft went under me. As he passed under me, I immediately did a steep left turn and came round inside the enemy aircraft, who was turning left. I finished some ten yards or less behind his tail, and the pilot looked over his left shoulder, half-rolled and went down vertically. I held my height – perhaps 1500 ft – above the ground and saw the Albatros flatten out at tree-top height and fly "on the carpet" due east.

'At this moment I realised that my engine was running very rough, running on three, five, seven and nine cylinders with great irregularity. The tappet rods had been damaged and the ignition wires cut in several places, shorting the plugs. The rotary engine had proved to be a good shield. Looking around, I saw fabric on the lower plane's leading edges torn and flapping in the breeze. I limped back to our side of the lines and to No 45 Sqn's aerodrome at Grossa, taking a last look at Hand's burning machine on the hillside.

'Later, I realised that the sound advice my CO, Maj A M Vaucour, had given me upon my arrival on the squadron had proved successful;

'"Never break formation, and should you find yourself alone in the middle of the enemy during a fight, turn straight at the first

enemy machine you see and fly for a collision – and never give way."'

Canadian Earl Hand survived being shot down by Linke-Crawford, although he suffered terrible burns to his left hand and back. Post-war, Hand told Huins that he had been visited in hospital by Linke-Crawford, and 'from Hand's description, he was a chivalrous type, and he wished "Handie" a full recovery'.

PILOT BIOGRAPHY – FRANK LINKE-CRAWFORD

Frank Linke-Crawford, who was born on 18 August 1893 in Krakau, Poland, was the son of Maj Adalbert Linke and his English-born wife Lucy Crawford. In 1910 Linke-Crawford entered the military academy at Wiener-Neustadt, in Austria, and three years later he graduated with the rank of lieutenant. Posted to Dragoon Regiment Nr 6, he was serving in the 1st *Eskadron* (cavalry troop) of this unit when war broke out in August 1914. Seeing combat and rising through the ranks, Linke-Crawford had received several decorations by the time he applied to join the *kaiserliche und königliche Luftfahrtruppen* (LFT) in December 1915. As an officer, he was considered for observer training, as 'chauffeuring' aircraft was deemed to be a job fit for non-commissioned officers only.

In March 1916 Linke-Crawford was posted to the newly-formed *Flik* 22, and after completing many sorties he was finally given permission to train as a pilot six months later – by then the role of the pilot had become better appreciated in the LFT. Completing his training in January 1917, Linke-Crawford was posted to *Flik* 12 on the Isonzo Front in northeastern Italy as deputy CO. Flying bombing and reconnaissance sorties in two-seat machines and fighter escort in single-seaters, he soon gained a reputation as an aggressive and determined pilot.

On 4 August he was reassigned to fighter squadron *Flik* 41J, based east of Trieste. The unit flew a mix of Albatros D III and Hansa-Brandenburg D I machines, and Linke-Crawford used one of the latter to claim his first victory on 21 August. He became an ace on 23 September with the destruction of an Italian flying boat, and by the time he was given command of *Flik* 60J in December, his score stood at 13. Now flying Phönix D Is, Linke-Crawford's unit engaged Italian, British and French types during the early months of 1918, with the CO claiming a further six victories on the type. Having been based near Grigno in the Val Sugana, some 60 miles north of Venice, *Flik* 60J moved to Feltre, east of Grigno, in March, where it received a number of agile, and fragile, Aviatik D Is to supplement the obsolescent Phönix machines.

Linke-Crawford continued to add victories to his tally in the spring and early summer, and by 29 July his score stood at 26. That day he claimed his 27th victim when he sent down a British two-seater in flames near Valstagna while flying Aviatik D I 115.32. Two days later, again patrolling in 115.32, Linke-Crawford became separated from his three compatriots following an engagement with a trio of Camels. He then ran into two Italian HD 1 fighters, and minutes later his D I was seen to spin down (suggesting a wing failure – a common occurrence with the Aviatik scout), before recovering and being attacked by the HD 1 flown by Caporale Aldo Astolfi. Linke-Crawford's machine came apart in the air, and the fourth ranking Austro-Hungarian ace fell to his death.

SPECIFICATION

Phönix D I

TYPE:	single-seat, single-engined biplane fighter
ACCOMMODATION:	one pilot
DIMENSIONS:	length 22 ft 1.75 in (6.75 m)
	wingspan 32 ft 1.80 in (9.80 m)
	height 8 ft 8.33 in (2.65 m)
WEIGHTS:	empty 1578 lb (716 kg)
	maximum take-off 2096 lb (951 kg)
PERFORMANCE:	maximum speed 111 mph (178 kmh)
	range, endurance of 1.5 hours
	powerplant Hiero
	output 200 hp (149 kW)
ARMAMENT:	two fixed Schwarzlose 8 mm machine guns immediately forward of the cockpit
FIRST FLIGHT DATE:	summer 1917
OPERATOR:	Austria-Hungary
PRODUCTION:	140

The first design by the Austro-Hungarian Phönix-Flugzeugwerke (which had previously been Albatros' subsidiary within the empire) to reach series production, the D I was the end result of three previous development designs, numbered 20.14, .15 and .16, which had flown between December 1916 and June 1917. These machines had in turn been influenced by the German Brandenburg D I 'star strutter', as well as captured Italian Nieuports. Like the latter aircraft, all three Phönix prototypes featured a sesquiplane wing layout, but they had failed to impress the Austro-Hungarian pilots with either their performance or their structural integrity. Phönix reverted to a traditional Sparmann-designed biplane cellule for the D I, producing engineering drawings for a machine based on the 20.15 and the re-winged 20.16 in June 1917. The first 11 aircraft were accepted by the LFT in October 1917, and production continued through to the late spring of 1918, by which time 120 had been built – a further 20 were also supplied to the Austro-Hungarian Navy. Although the D I was slower than many of its contemporaries, it remained a frontline fighter until the Armistice. Indeed, pilots appreciated the scout's sturdiness and excellent handling characteristics.

Oeffag-built Albatros D III 153.11 of Oberleutnant Frank Linke-Crawford, *Flik* 41J, Sesana, October 1917

Having wangled his way into the elite *Flik* 41J in August 1917, Linke-Crawford achieved his early victories in a Phönix-built Brandenburg D I, before transferring to this Albatros D III in October. He claimed five kills in this machine between 23 October and 23 November 1917.

FOKKER ACE

'I pulled my Fokker straight up, and for one advantageous moment I had the SE 5 squarely in front of my guns.'

Carl Degelow celebrates his awarding of the Knight's Cross of the Royal Hohenzollern House Order, seen above his left tunic pocket, and is pictured here with his 'white stag' D VII. The stag has golden yellow hooves and antlers. The pale rib tapes are quite evident on the five-colour fabric wing covering, and a tubular gunsight is mounted between the guns (*via Greg VanWyngarden*)

On the evening of 24 September 1918, Leutnant Carl Degelow, commander of *Jagdstaffel* 40, led his pilots against ten Armstrong Whitworth FK 8 bombers of No 82 Sqn RAF, escorted by SE 5a fighters of No 41 Sqn. The Fokker D VIIs climbed to attack the higher-flying escorts. In his memoirs *Germany's Last Knight of the Air - The Memoirs of Major Carl Degelow*, translated and edited by Peter Kilduff, Degelow wrote;

'Toward evening the *Staffel* would start out on patrol. We knew from experience that at this time of day British bombing squadrons would cross our lines in an attempt to saturate strategic points in the army sector with their dangerous cargo. To stop them, we would have to catch them unawares, and our approach flight was arranged accordingly. We knew they would expect us to attack from above, so we would alternate our plan and put off "making altitude", as we called it whenever we tried to reach great heights of 5000 metres or so, and catch them from below.

'Such flights during clear weather were always a pleasure, offering no better sport. We could fly a wide course, looking for our prey. Now came a reconnoitring and searching of the heavens for enemy aircraft. Puffs of anti-aircraft smoke in the distance were enough to tell even the novice that intruders were over our territory.

'During such a flight on the evening of 24 September we came upon an enemy bombing squadron near Menin. The flight consisted of ten bombing aircraft protected by eight single-seaters. Our tactic was to first attack the fighters, since they flew higher then their bomb-laden companions. We gained altitude and caught the British SE 5s from the least expected point – right beneath their floorboards. I closed in on a fellow with a big white "Y" painted on his top wing. This "Mister Y" was a very skilful flier, and he avoided my attack through a series of very deft turns.

'Nothing I did could entice him to come down to my level. So, after we had wildly stormed round and round each other a few times, I tried to bluff him. I pulled my Fokker straight up, and for one advantageous moment I had the SE 5 squarely in front of my guns. I pressed the buttons of my machine guns, really only to intimidate my partner by the fire, and hopefully get him to give up his advantageous altitude and dive for the ground. But, in so doing, some of my shots, which were surely accidental hits, went into the reserve fuel tank of the enemy aircraft.

'Bright flames immediately burst from the emergency fuel supply on the top wing, where it was located on the SE. I was very pleased by my bluff, and believed the enemy now to be finished. "Mister Y" had, however, pulled far away, as there was no way for him to bring the aerial battle to a favourable end. Then, with his machine glowing with fire, he dived right at me, all the while maintaining a murderous stream of fire from his machine guns. I must say that this unexpected attack upset me, to put it mildly, but at the same time the fellow's foolhardiness aroused my fighting spirit.

Carl Degelow (fourth from right in light-coloured tunic) is pictured with his pilots in front of their black *Jasta* 40 warbirds. The first five D VIIs from the right have been identified as Degelow's machine, with its stag and white diagonal stripe on the upper wing, Rosenstein's, with a white chord-wise stripe, Jeschonnek's with a rampant bull, Gilly's, with its white swastika and Frodien's, with a hawk's head (*via Greg VanWyngarden*)

'The Englishman suddenly made a violent dive, during which the rush of air almost snuffed out the inferno over his head. But as soon as he resumed level flight, the fire broke out with great intensity. After a last futile attack, and recognising the hopelessness of continued fighting, he decided to withdraw from the encounter and tried to slip away from me. But I was not yet ready to give up

the fight. I pursued him doggedly, and was soon joined by another gentleman of my *Staffel*, who added a few shots to the effort to ensure that "Mister Y" did not reach his lines intact. Severely battered by our attack, the enemy aircraft exploded at low altitude and broke up close to the edge of Zillebeke Lake.'

Despite Carl Degelow's mistaken belief, his opponent, Capt C Crawford of No 41 Sqn RAF, somehow survived the absolute destruction of his fighting scout to be taken prisoner by German troops.

High spirits in the *Jasta* 40 Officer's Kasino as the *Staffelführer* is placed under severe 'threat'. Seated, from left to right, are Hermann Gilly, Carl Degelow, Hans Jeschonnek, Willy Rosenstein and Frodien (*via Greg VanWyngarden*)

PILOT BIOGRAPHY – CARL DEGELOW

Carl Degelow was born in January 1891 in Müsterdorf. Pre-war, he had worked in the USA as an industrial chemist, and therefore spoke English well. Degelow returned to Germany shortly before the outbreak of war to enlist in the second Nassauischen Infanterie-Regiment Nr 88, seeing action in France and Russia. Commissioned in July 1915, he transferred to the aviation service the following year, and was sent to Fl. Abt. (A) 216 on the Somme at the beginning of 1917. Degelow's aggressive flying got him moved to fighters, and *Jasta* 7, and by mid-May 1918 he had scored a handful of victories prior to his transfer to *Jasta* 40. After the death, on 9 July, of previous leader Helmuth Dilthey, Degelow took over the unit.

He picked up his first Fokker D VII on 25 June 1918. After having *Staffel* mechanics check it over and load the ammunition, Degelow took it up for a brief hop. During this 'test flight' he encountered a scrap between Camels and D VIIs of another *Jasta*, and duly downed a Sopwith attacking one of the Fokkers – it was his sixth victory. Degelow's claims from July onwards were attained with the D VII, six aircraft falling to his guns in that first month. He was on leave in August, but added six more victories in September, ten in October and one – his 30th and last – on 4 November.

Degelow survived the war to write a short memoir, *Mit dem weissen Hirsch durch dick und dünn (With the White Stag through Thick and Thin)*. In 1979, nine years after Degelow's death, historian Peter Kilduff expanded on this work, using extensive interviews and additional material to produce *Germany's Last Knight of the Air*, which provides an excellent view of 4th Army D VII operations.

SPECIFICATION

Fokker D VII

TYPE: single-seat, single-engined biplane fighter

ACCOMMODATION: one pilot

DIMENSIONS: length 22 ft 9.66 in (6.95 m)
wingspan 29 ft 2.333 in (8.90 m)
height 9 ft 0 in (2.75 m)

WEIGHTS: empty 1508 lb (684 kg)
maximum take-off 2006 lb (910 kg)

PERFORMANCE: maximum speed 116 mph (187 kmh)
range, endurance of 1.5 hours
powerplant Mercedes D IIIaü
output 180 hp (134 kW)

ARMAMENT: two fixed Maxim LMG 08/15 7.92 mm machine guns immediately forward of the cockpit

FIRST FLIGHT DATE: December 1917

OPERATOR: Germany

PRODUCTION: 2000+

The arrival of the Fokker D VII at the front in late April 1918 finally began to redress the balance in favour of the German Air Service, whose pilots had had to fly obsolete Albatros D V, D Va and Pfalz D IIIs against superior Allied types such as the SE 5a, Sopwith Triplane and Camel, Bristol F 2B, the French SPAD VII and later SPAD XIII. The battle for air supremacy over the trenches was paramount to both sides so that their armies could launch assaults with support from the air. Fokker's Dr I had briefly redressed the balance in late 1917, yet even Manfred von Richthofen was fully aware that the life of the triplane was limited, and a new machine was desperately needed. He was among the aces who had tested the new Fokker biplane prototype, and was eager to see its arrival at the front. Indeed, one of the last things he did prior to his death in action on 21 April 1918 was write to the German Air Service High Command seeking news on the availability of the D VII. 'After a long time I come once again with a question. When can I count on the arrival of Fokker biplanes with the super-compressed engines? The superiority of British single-seat and reconnaissance aircraft makes it even more perceptibly unpleasant here. The single-seaters fight coming over at high altitude and stay there. One cannot even shoot at them. Speed is the most important point. One could shoot down five to ten times as many if we were faster. Please give me news soon about when we can count on these new machines.'

Fokker D VII (Alb) of Ltn d R Carl Degelow, *Jasta* 40, Lomme, August 1918

Jasta 40's D VIIs all sported black fuselages, augmented by a white tail unit. Cabane and landing gear struts and wheel covers were also black. The wings of this Albatros-built D VII are covered in five-colour fabric, with blue rib tapes and a diagonal white stripe on the top wing to identify the *Staffelführer*. Degelow's 'white stag' emblem displays golden yellow antlers and hooves.

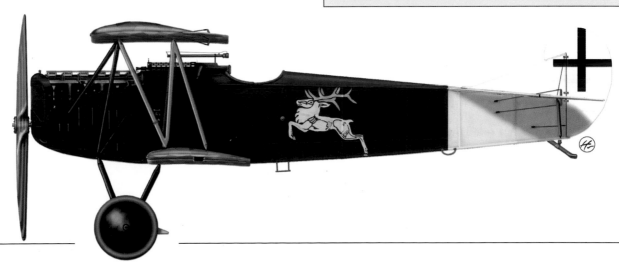

'BALLOON-BUSTER'

'Once ignited, a burning balloon could be seen for miles, assuring confirmation for the fighter pilot who destroyed it — provided he returned to claim the kill.'

At 0720 hrs on the morning of 15 August 1918, American Lt Edgar Taylor from Central Falls, Rhode Island, claimed a kite balloon shot down in flames over Estaires for his second victory. He would destroy a further three *Drachens* ('dragons', an Austrian analogy for Chinese kites) prior to his death in combat just nine days later. Taylor had been transferred to No 79 Sqn at Beauvois, in France, in April 1918, but had been a slow starter. Indeed, he had failed to gain his first victory until 4 August, when he destroyed a Fokker D VII. Taylor then took on the challenge of balloon-busting, destroying four of these dangerous targets during the same month, but in the process of claiming his last victim near Sailly sur la Lys on the 24th, he was hit by ground fire and mortally wounded.

Edgar Taylor has no known grave, and he was just 20 years of age when he died of his injuries, possibly in German hands, the day after claiming his fifth victim to 'make ace'.

Captive or kite balloons, also known as *Drachens* and 'Sausages', were the oldest form of aerial reconnaissance, first being used by the French in 1795. They saw considerable use during World War 1, since they could stay in the air longer than aeroplanes and, thanks to their stabilising fins, they provided the observer with a

This official Sopwith factory photograph of a fully armed Dolphin was taken on 15 February 1918. Note the muzzles of the twin Vickers 0.303-in machine guns immediately forward of the cockpit, and the angled Lewis guns above them *(via Norman Franks)*

This line up of No 79 Sqn Dolphins was photographed at Bickendorf, near Köln, in early 1919, the unit seeing service with the Army of Occupation in Germany until being disbanded on 15 July that same year. The aircraft closest to the camera (C8189) was used by Capt F J Stevenson to claim three victories in the last week of the war, while E4756 was the final mount of 17-victory ace Capt Ronald Bannerman (via Norman Franks)

steady platform from which to scan a large portion of the frontlines. Communicating by telephone with forces on the ground, the balloon observers could direct artillery or detect frontline movements, and as such, they constituted a very real menace to the other side's troops. Destroying enemy balloons, therefore, was a very desirable objective before a major offensive, defensive or logistic support operation was to be carried out.

On the face of it, a large bag filled with hydrogen would seem an easy target for an enterprising fighter pilot, but most airmen regarded balloon-busting missions as extraordinarily difficult and dangerous. The balloons were located deep within enemy lines, requiring their attackers to go after them, exposed to observation, fighters and every enemy soldier carrying a gun.

Although the balloon floated several thousand feet above the ground, it could be rapidly brought down by means of a powered winch when attacked, while a cordon of anti-aircraft guns surrounded it with a descending cone of fire through which the attacking fighter had to dive. Once the pilot reached the balloon, he would find it surprisingly difficult to ignite pure hydrogen, even with incendiary bullets. Only by pouring a sustained burst into the 'gas bag', allowing some hydrogen to escape and mix with the oxygen, could the attacking pilot hope to create the fire that, once started, would quickly consume the entire balloon.

Once ignited, a burning balloon could be seen for miles, assuring confirmation for the fighter pilot who destroyed it – provided he returned to claim the kill. But the pyre was equally visible to the enemy, and the balloon-buster faced a gauntlet of anti-aircraft and ground fire, as well as vengeful enemy fighters converging on his most likely escape route.

Taken in sum, those factors rendered balloon-busting a suicide mission, requiring as much luck as skill on the pilot's part, and an aeroplane capable of standing up to considerable punishment. French ace of aces René Fonck, who hated leaving anything to chance, did not include a single balloon among his 75 victories, stating in no uncertain terms that 'I do not thus like to combat the enemy, and I prefer to leave it to the specialists of such attacks'. The few airmen who made a practice of volunteering for anti-*Drachen* missions were regarded as something of a special breed, possessed of a combination of pyromania and a latent death wish known as 'balloon fever'.

No 79 Sqn Dolphin F7065 was also photographed at Bickendorf during the unit's time with the Army of Occupation. Lt Edgar Taylor's Dolphin D3727 was identically marked to this machine, although it carried the individual letter 'J' instead of 'U' (via Norman Franks)

PILOT BIOGRAPHY – EDGAR TAYLOR

One of a number of American citizens to see action with the RFC/RAF and RNAS rather than the US Air Service, despite the US declaration of war with Germany in 1917, Edgar Taylor of Central Falls, Rhode Island, joined the RFC in early 1918. After earning his wings, he was posted to No 79 Sqn at Beauvois in April. The unit had been assigned to frontline flying just a matter of weeks before, equipped with the then new Sopwith Dolphin.

After a slow start, Taylor gained his first victory on 4 August, when he destroyed a Fokker D VII. He then destroyed four balloons during the same month, but in the process of claiming his last victim on the 24th, he was hit by ground fire and mortally wounded.

Rare photographs of American ace Edgar Taylor (*via Norman Franks*)

Dolphin D3727 of Lt Edgar Taylor, No 79 Sqn, Ste-Marie-Cappel, August 1918
American Lt Edgar Taylor gained all five of his victories with D3727, and he was also mortally wounded at its controls. Marked with the identification letter 'J' aft of the unit's white square marking, which was repeated on the top port wing inboard of the roundel, this aircraft served with No 79 Sqn from 16 June to 24 August 1918, when it was lost in action. D3727 had completed 97 flying hours prior to its final sortie.

SPECIFICATION

Sopwith Dolphin

TYPE: single-seat, single-engined biplane fighter

ACCOMMODATION: one pilot

DIMENSIONS: length 22 ft 3 in (6.78 m)
wingspan 32 ft 6 in (9.90 m)
height 8 ft 6 in (2.59 m)

WEIGHTS: empty 1466 lb (665 kg)
maximum take-off 2000 lb (907 kg)

PERFORMANCE: maximum speed 128 mph (206 kmh)
range 195 miles (315 km)
powerplant Hispano-Suiza 8E
output 200 hp (149 kW)

ARMAMENT: two fixed Vickers 0.303-in machine guns immediately forward of the cockpit and one or two moveable Lewis 0.303-in machine guns mounted over the top wing

FIRST FLIGHT DATE: May 1917

OPERATOR: UK

PRODUCTION: 1532

Built as a Camel replacement, the Dolphin was unique in that it was the first multi-gun fighter to see action during World War 1. It was also the first active Sopwith machine not to be fitted with a rotary engine. The Dolphin was designed with two belt-fed 0.303-in Vickers guns mounted in front of the windscreen in the pilot's line of sight, and it was also capable of having two drum-fed 0.303-in Lewis guns fixed to the cockpit cross-member connecting the two upper wings. When Sopwith's chief designer Herbert Smith was tasked with creating the Dolphin in the spring of 1917, he determined to produce a machine that gave its pilot the best possible all-round visibility. He achieved this by putting the pilot's eye-line above the upper wings. To further improve visibility downwards, he removed the centre section from the upper wings and back-staggered them by 13 inches in comparison with the lower wings. As he had done with the Camel, Smith designed his new machine with all its mass – engine, guns, petrol tank and pilot – grouped together 'up front', so that the Dolphin would inherit the high degree of manoeuvrability associated with his previous Sopwith fighting scout. The first production examples reached No 19 Sqn in the final week of 1917, and by 9 January 1918 the unit had exchanged all of its SPAD VIIs for Dolphins. The aircraft flew its first combat patrol on 3 February, and by month-end the Dolphin had claimed its first victories.

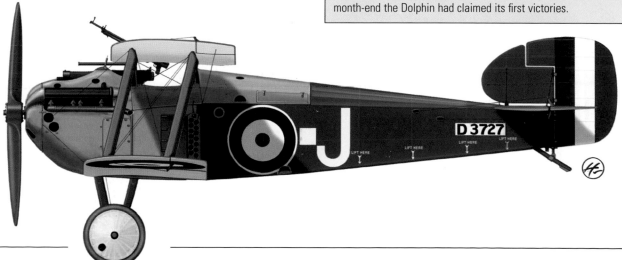

'SHOOTING STAR'

'An unfortunate Boche got in the way of some American-made bullets and burst into flames.'

On 23 October 1918, 1Lt Jacques Michael Swaab of the 22nd Aero Squadron was conducting a patrol of the front when he spotted a burning blimp of the 7th Balloon Company falling near Cierges. Breaking formation to give chase to the Fokker D VII that had just set the 'gas bag' alight, he finally brought his quarry down in flames behind German lines near Thenorgues. His opponent was Leutnant Max Näther of *Jagdstaffel* 62, who miraculously survived being shot down uninjured, and added the balloon to his eventual wartime total of 26 victories. While trying to rejoin his formation, Swaab encountered a Rumpler two-seater and shot it down as well, taking his tally to six.

The American was flying Kellner-built SPAD XIII S7640, which bore the name *MAYER II* beneath its cockpit in honour of the pilot's father. Swaab's final score of ten victories made him the 'Shooting Star' of the 22nd Aero Squadron.

Swaab's stellar career as a fighter pilot had gotten off to a shaky start. Completing his training at Issoudun, in France, he begged American test pilot Temple Joyce to arrange for him to serve alongside him, insisting that he needed more flying time before he felt ready for combat. On his first day as a test pilot, however, Swaab made a perfect landing ten feet above the ground, then pancaked, writing off his aeroplane. On the third day he ground-looped, breaking both the wings of yet another machine. After that, Joyce's commander told him, 'For God's sake, send that idiot up to the front. He's safer there than he is back here'!

When Swaab flew his first patrol on 8 September, he balked when his flight went into an almost vertical dive – up to that

After a shaky start as a test pilot, 1Lt Jacques Michael Swaab had little confidence in his ability to fly fighters, but he not only survived his first combat, on 8 September 1918, but returned with three Fokker scouts to his credit. Swaab went on to down seven more enemy aeroplanes to finish the war as the 'shooting star' of the 22nd Aero Squadron *(via Norman Franks)*

Blériot-built SPAD XIII S18869 'Red 15' was assigned to 1Lt Jacques Michael Swaab on 3 November 1918 after he turned in war-weary SPAD XIII S7640 'Red 7', which he had used to score most of his victories. Like Swaab's previous two SPADs, he named this 22nd Aero Squadron machine *MAYER III* after his father (*via Jon Guttman*)

Swaab's SPAD XIII S18869 is seen here at Vosges, in France, in March 1919, by which point the ten German crosses which surrounded the comet insignia of the 22nd Aero Squadron had been removed. Swaab himself is standing alongside the fighter's cockpit (*via Jon Guttman*)

point he had flown Nieuports, with instructions not to exceed 120 mph in a dive, and nobody had told him that the SPAD XIII was a much sturdier machine. Descending at a more prudent speed, Swaab found himself alone, so he flew west for 20 minutes until he spotted an airfield. He wrote his own unofficial account of what followed in his diary:

'I shot through the clouds, and there before me was an airdrome, and not an aeroplane in sight. Prudence told me to go down slowly. Then, when 200 metres from the field, my eyes almost popped out of my head when I saw a Fokker (the first for me) rising from the field at right angles to me.

'Just about this moment I said "au revoir" to myself in my best French (the last I expected to use for some time) and dove at the Fokker, opening fire with both guns – one of which jammed! But what a glorious sight I saw! Flames burst out all over the aeroplane, and I circled it and saw it crash in flames. Four million, seven hundred thousand machine guns then chased me off the field, soon to be followed by "onions" and "archies", which came damnably close when flying at a few hundred metres.

'Oh, friendly sun! Every time I managed to get a look at it through the clouds, it had moved further away. Finally, I managed to mount through the clouds, and for a few miles I almost enjoyed myself. Shading my eyes against "Old Sol", I saw a wing – a very unfriendly wing, at which I fired.

'A Fokker made a steep spiral and ended in a steep nose dive. The next instant, I saw that a group of about ten Fokkers had enticed me into a game of "ring-around-the-rosy", in which the object seemed to be for each one in turn to practice aerial gunnery on me! Fortune permitted me to get closer and closer to a cloud, when one chap who worked for "Buffalo Bill" shooting

pennies off a blind man's head, mistook me for his "old partner" and missed, gently touching my scalp with three bullets.

'The cloud had come closer to me and I headed for it when an unfortunate Boche got in the way of some American-made bullets and burst into flames. I made the cloud – vrilled a billion metres, three times, passed away into semi-consciousness and next found myself pinned under my aeroplane.

'French was being spoken! The people argued about my nationality, forgetting that the aeroplane's occupant needed assistance until they were awakened by my saying, "Lever ici"! I knew that phrase perfectly – a year of seeing it on every machine had impressed it in my mind. They lifted the aeroplane. I fell out, and crawled from under it. "Hurry up with the ladder"! But why say more? Those first two words told me I was among friends – the ladder was to be used as a stretcher on which to carry me away for repairs.'

PILOT BIOGRAPHY – JACQUES SWAAB

Born on 21 April 1894, Jacques Michael Swaab was the son of Philadelphia businessman Mayer Swaab. Fellow ace and close friend Arthur Raymond Brooks remembered Swaab as being 'an excellent chap to be with, a well-bred fellow of good background, well taken care of by the ladies in the USA. He was suave and well-educated, Jewish, but not very religious'.

Joining the United States Air Service (USAS) soon after the American government entered the war on 6 April 1917, he completed his flying training at Issoudun in the late summer and then spent a brief spell flying as a test pilot for the USAS. Writing off two aeroplanes within days of his arrival, he was transferred to the recently-formed 22nd Aero Squadron on 27 August 1918. One of four units that made up the 2nd Pursuit Group, the 22nd was equipped with new SPAD XIIIs.

Swaab saw combat in all the major actions in which the squadron participated over the French/American front – namely the Toul, St Mihiel and Argonne offensives. His first patrol, on 8 September, was very nearly his last, as he became separated from his unit and was engaged by a number of Fokker D VIIs over a German airfield. He emerged from the clash with three victories, but was forced to crash-land when he lost consciousness after suffering a slight head wound. When he failed to return to base, Swaab was given up for lost by his squadronmates, until they learned of his ordeal two days later.

A formation of Bréguet 14B2s of the 96th Aero Squadron, returning from an aborted bombing mission, had witnessed his fight and confirmed his three victories. After hearing his account, Swaab's test pilot friend Temple Joyce asked, 'Jack, I can understand how you could just inadvertently figure the right deflection to get a guy, but why the devil didn't they get you?' 'Well, Temp', Swaab replied, 'you know I can't fly, and when the sons of guns aimed at me, I was either skidding or slipping, and never got to where they were firing!'

Continuing to claim victories during the autumn of 1918, Swaab scored his final success on 31 October when he chased an LVG bomber over the frontline before his bullets struck home and it exploded in mid-air east of Verdun. That brought Swaab's total to ten, making him the leading ace of the 22nd Aero Squadron.

Post-war, Swaab found employment working in the motion picture business in Hollywood, where he served as the technical adviser to the film *Dawn Patrol*, starring Errol Flynn and David Niven. He died in Los Angeles on 7 July 1963 and was buried in the Arlington Military Cemetery in Washington, DC.

SPECIFICATION

SPAD XIII

TYPE:	single-seat, single-engined biplane fighter
ACCOMMODATION:	one pilot
DIMENSIONS:	length 20 ft 6 in (6.25 m)
	wingspan 27 ft 1 in (8.25 m)
	height 8 ft 6.5 in (2.60 m)
WEIGHTS:	empty 1326 lb (601 kg)
	maximum take-off 1888 lb (856 kg)
PERFORMANCE:	maximum speed 135 mph (218 kmh)
	range, endurance of 1.67 hours
	powerplant Hispano-Suiza 8B
	output 200 hp (149 kW)
ARMAMENT:	two fixed Vickers 7.7 mm machine guns
	immediately forward of the cockpit
FIRST FLIGHT:	4 April 1917
OPERATORS:	France, UK, Italy, Belgium, USA
PRODUCTION:	8470

Derived from the highly successful SPAD VII and limited-edition XII, the XIII was developed to make use of the powerful Hispano-Suiza 8B engine, which cranked out 200 hp. Dubbed the 'geared SPAD' due to the arrangement of its powerplant, the XIII bore a striking resemblance to the earlier VII, but was larger overall. The extra performance offered by the 8B engine allowed company designers to fit two 7.7 mm Vickers guns into the XIII, and the *Aviation Militaire* enthusiastically ordered 8470 examples to be built. However, a combination of manufacturing problems and chronic engine reliability drastically slowed the delivery process, and of the 2200 XIIIs promised by SPAD for completion by March 1918, just 764 had been built, of which only 300 were in operational service. With the engine woes eventually rectified, production finally began to meet demand in the late spring of 1918, SPAD churning out 11 XIIIs a day until manufacturing ceased in 1919. By then some 8470 aircraft had been built, and aside from its use by French *Escadrilles*, British, Italian, Belgian and American units also saw action with the SPAD.

SPAD XIII S18869 of Capt Jacques Swaab, 22nd Aero Squadron, November 1918
Swaab was issued with this Blériot-built SPAD XIII after he claimed all of his ten victories during the autumn of 1918. His first three came on 8 September, when he downed a trio of D VIIs over their airfield. His final victory – an LVG bomber – was claimed on 31 October near Verdun. His fighter, assigned to him as a replacement for war-weary SPAD XIII S7640, was marked in standard squadron colours, featuring a blue, red and yellow comet. The ten black crosses surrounding the unit emblem were a rare example of victory markings applied to a World War 1 fighter.

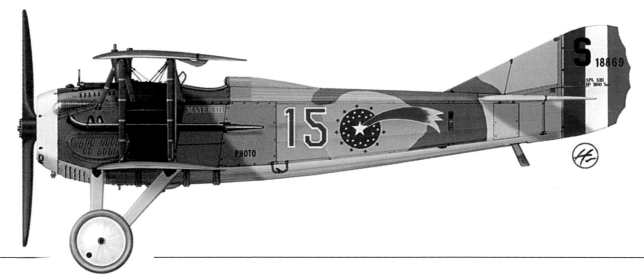

Barker's Battle

'He then found himself in the middle of a large formation of Fokkers, who attacked him from all directions.'

Although only seeing combat on the Western Front for the last few months of the war, the Sopwith Snipe was involved in one of the most famous engagements of the conflict on 27 October 1918. The central character in this epic dogfight was leading Italian Front ace Maj W G 'Billy' Barker, who had claimed 42 victories flying Camels with No 28 Sqn by the time he returned to England in September.

The Canadian ace could have easily seen out the rest of the conflict as an instructor, but he managed to convince his superiors to send him to France in order to gain up-to-date knowledge of the air fighting on the Western Front which he could in turn impart to his students. Barker was duly attached to Camel-equipped No 201 Sqn, although he took a brand new Sopwith Snipe with him in order to evaluate its capabilities in combat.

He flew with the unit from Beugnâtre for two weeks, but he had failed to see any combat by the time he took off on his last patrol on 27 October 1918. The official citation for Barker's Victoria Cross reveals what happened next;

'On the morning of 27 October 1918, this officer observed an enemy two-seater over the Forét de Mornal. He attacked this machine, and after a short burst it broke up in the air. At the same time a Fokker biplane attacked him and he was wounded in the right thigh, but he managed despite this to shoot down the enemy aeroplane in flames.

'He then found himself in the middle of a large formation of Fokkers, who attacked him from all directions and again wounded him in the left thigh, although he succeeded in driving down two of the enemy in a spin.

Maj 'Billy' Barker fought in France and Italy, amassing claims for 46 victories, including nine balloons. Returning to France late in the war, he was credited with four more successes in his final engagement on 27 October 1918. This epic clash with a large number of Fokker D VIIs finally ended when he was shot down and badly wounded (*via Norman Franks*)

'He lost consciousness after this, and his machine fell out of control. On recovery, he found himself again being attacked, but, notwithstanding that he was now severely wounded in both legs and his left arm was shattered, he dived on the nearest machine and shot it down in flames.

'Being greatly exhausted, he dived out of the fight to regain our lines, but was met by another formation, which attacked and endeavoured to cut him off, but after a hard fight he succeeded in breaking up this formation and reached our lines, where he crashed on landing.

'This combat, in which Maj Barker destroyed four enemy machines (three of them in flames), brought his total successes up to 50 enemy aeroplanes destroyed, and is a notable example of exceptional bravery and disregard of danger which this very

gallant officer has always displayed throughout his distinguished career.

'Maj Barker was awarded the Military Cross on 10 January 1917, his first Bar on 18 July 1917, the Distinguished Service Cross on 18 February 1918, the second Bar to his Military Cross on 16 September 1918 and the Bar to his Distinguished Service Order on 2 November 1918.'

Having recovered from his wounds, Barker was always reticent to discuss this engagement, some say because of his modesty, or perhaps he was mindful that he had made a mistake and been caught napping. That he himself felt that he had not deserved the acclaim, or the award of Britain's highest military medal, is another matter. Barker would talk of his more – to him – heroic escapades in Italy.

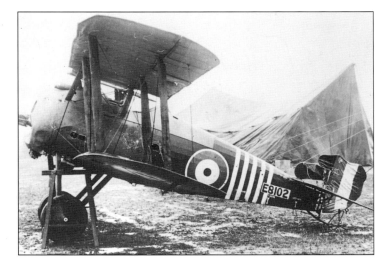

Sopwith Snipe E8102 was the aircraft in which Maj Barker won his VC in a single-handed action on 27 October 1918. Note the scout's crushed tail fin and engine cowling following his crash-landing. The white bar markings are similar to those used by Barker to decorate his Camel in Italy earlier in the war (*via Norman Franks*)

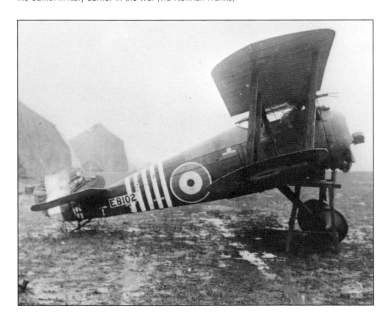

Maj Barker poses with a souvenir from one of his victims during 1918 (*via Norman Franks*)

A view of the starboard side of Maj Barker's Snipe. The main section of the fuselage of this machine is a prized exhibit in the Canadian War Museum in Ottawa (*via Norman Franks*)

PILOT BIOGRAPHY – WILLIAM 'BILLY' BARKER

The amazing William George 'Billy' Barker was born in Dauphin, Manitoba, on 3 November 1894. As a youth, he became an accomplished horseman and an excellent shot with a rifle. The eve of World War 1 found Barker living in Winnipeg, and in November 1914 he enlisted in the 1st Battalion of the Canadian Mounted Rifles as a private. By the time he arrived in France, via England, Barker had already applied to join the RFC. He saw brief action in the trenches prior to training as an observer and being posted to No 9 Sqn, which was equipped with BE 2s. Serving with similarly-equipped Nos 4 and 15 Sqns in France, Barker then retrained as a pilot and returned to No 15 Sqn in early 1917. While flying BE 2s, he won a Bar to the Military Cross (MC) that he had been awarded when serving as an observer.

Having tasted aerial combat, Barker asked for a transfer to single-seat fighters and was sent to No 28 Sqn, which was equipped with Camels. Soon becoming a flight commander, he scored three victories in France and then a further 19 in Italy following the unit's transfer to the Italian Front in November 1917. Barker then moved to No 66 Sqn, again as flight commander, and added 16 more victories to his tally, gaining a second Bar to his MC, plus a DSO and the Italian Silver Medal. Given command of No 139 Sqn, which flew Bristol F2b fighters, he took his Camel with him, and with it brought his score to 46, for which he was awarded a Bar to his DSO.

Returning to England as an instructor in September 1918, Barker managed to persuade his superiors to allow him a short period in France to bring himself up to date with the latest developments, and in a famous action on 27 October, was credited with four victories. He was severely wounded in this dogfight, however, although it brought him the award of the Victoria Cross.

After the war Barker went into civil aviation and then served in the Royal Canadian Air Force until 1924. Returning to civilian life to start a tobacco business, he was made vice president of the Fairchild Aviation Corporation of Canada in early 1930 and was killed when the Fairchild KR-21 that he was flying crashed at Rockcliffe aerodrome, Ottawa, on 12 March that same year.

Snipe E8102 of Maj 'Billy' Barker, attached to No 201 Sqn, Beugnâtre, October 1918
This is the famous Snipe flown by Barker during his attachment to No 201 Sqn in France. His personal markings consisted of five thin white bands around the rear fuselage aft of the roundel, this decoration partially reflecting the markings he carried on the Camel that he flew in Italy. The latter machine boasted seven white and six black bands in roughly the same area. Another feature of his Italian Front Camel that was also present on the Snipe was a small, red, flat-metal devil thumbing his nose with both hands, which was affixed to the front of the starboard Vickers machine gun.

SPECIFICATION

Sopwith Snipe

TYPE:	single-seat, single-engined biplane fighter
ACCOMMODATION:	one pilot
DIMENSIONS:	length 19 ft 10 in (6.04 m)
	wingspan 31 ft 1 in (9.47 m)
	height 8 ft 3 in (2.51 m)
WEIGHTS:	empty 1312 lb (595 kg)
	maximum take-off 2020 lb (916 kg)
PERFORMANCE:	maximum speed 121 mph (195 kmh)
	range, endurance of 3 hours
	powerplant Bentley BR2
	output 234 hp (172 kW)
ARMAMENT:	two fixed Vickers 0.303-in machine guns
	immediately forward of the cockpit
FIRST FLIGHT:	September 1917
OPERATOR:	UK
PRODUCTION:	1100

Conceived as a replacement for the Camel, and designed from specifications given to Sopwith by the Air Board in early 1917, the Snipe looked every bit the big brother of the company's famed fighting scout. The specification called for a fighter that could attain 135 mph at 15,000 ft, sustain an average rate of climb of 1000 ft per minute above 10,000 ft and cruise at 25,000 ft. The aircraft also had to have an endurance of three hours. Once in service, the Snipe proved unable to reproduce any of these figures, despite being powered by the 230 hp Bentley BR2 engine. Ignoring these shortcomings, the RAF voiced its approval of the machine, and the Snipe was put into large-scale production. Of the 4500 ordcrcd, 487 had been built by the end of December 1918, and production continued into the early 1920s. Examples started to arrive in France in August 1918, and No 43 Sqn was the first to swap its Camels for Snipes. The Australian Flying Corps' No 4 Sqn followed suit in October, and the final unit to receive examples prior to the Armistice was No 208 Sqn. Some 1100 Snipes were eventually built for the RAF, and the fighter remained in service until 1926.

DESERT DOGFIGHT

'I shouted "Tally Ho!" and dived on the rearmost flight, engaging the left hand man.'

Peter Wykeham-Barnes was one of the most successful fighter pilots of the early stages of the air war in North Africa, downing a number of Italian aircraft in the second half of 1940 (*via Norman Franks*)

On the evening of 4 August 1940, three Gladiators of No 80 Sqn left their advanced base at Sidi Barrani, on the Egyptian coast, to escort a Lysander of No 208 Sqn that had been ordered to conduct a reconnaissance overflight of Italian positions in the Bir Taieb el Esem area, some 30 miles inside the Libyan border. As the formation approached Sidi Omar, they found action, as recalled afterwards by Flg Off Peter Wykeham–Barnes:

'I flew at about 3000 ft above and behind the Lysander, with Sgt Rew on my right. About 4000 ft above and behind me were Flt Lt Pattle and Plt Off Lancaster. We reached our objective at approximately 1815 hrs, and as the Lysander turned over the enemy convoy, it was fired on, and dived away to the east. I attempted to locate the aircraft which had fired at it, but was unable to do so. I therefore turned east, and a moment or two later saw six Breda 65s flying west. I shouted "Tally Ho!" and dived on the rearmost flight, engaging the left hand man. Sgt Rew dived with me and engaged the right hand man of the same formation. I last saw him diving after his Breda, which had broken formation, and my Breda began to fall away to the left.

'At this moment two CR.32s came at me from above and in front, and at the same moment I thought I saw the remaining two Gladiators attacking. A general dogfight now took place, and I had shots at CR.32s from dead ahead and at every type of deflection. After about five minutes I got a CR.32 ahead of me, and was giving it a long burst, when my rudder went slack. I looked around and saw a CR.32 coming in on my beam, firing hard. A moment later my elevators went slack, and the machine fell onto an even keel, with no control. The CR.32 fell in behind me, and in a long burst from close range finished my aircraft off.

'The left side of the instrument panel and most of the windscreen went, and two bullets came through the back of the seat before I could close the throttle, and the CR.32 passed underneath me. My machine fell into a dive and I abandoned it, landing by parachute. On the way down, the Fiat passed within a few feet of me and fired, but I think not at me. When I picked myself up the Fiat was circling overhead at about 500 ft, but took no further action. I ran for about a mile from the machine, thinking I was in enemy territory, and on the way saw another

No 80 Sqn's first Gladiator kill was claimed by Flg Off Peter Wykeham-Barnes on 4 August 1940 in this aircraft (L8009/YK-I) when he downed a Ba.65 and a CR.32, before being shot down himself (*via Norman Franks*)

Gladiator I K8011 was also on strength with No 80 Sqn during Peter Wykeham-Barnes' time with the unit. Regularly flown by fellow ace Flg Off John Lapsley, it is seen here during a formation practice flight over Egypt in the spring of 1940 (*via Andrew Thomas*)

Gladiator spinning down, the pilot bailing out (this must have been Flt Lt "Pat" Pattle – author) at about 500 ft. He landed about two miles away and I did not see him again.

'I remained hidden until darkness, and then returned to the wreck to look for the water bottle, which was smashed. Retaining only my gun and overalls, I then set out on an easterly course, keeping away from the road. I crossed the wire at about 2230 hrs,

Aces in waiting! Three of No 80 Sqn's most notable pilots are seen in this photograph, taken at Amiriya, in Egypt, just before the outbreak of war with Italy. They are 'Tap' Jones (left), 'Pat' Pattle (centre) and Peter Wykeham-Barnes (right). Between them, these three aces would claim over 70 victories, of which around 50 were credited to South African Pattle, thus making him the most successful Commonwealth fighter pilot by some margin (*via Andrew Thomas*)

and at dawn altered course north and picked up the track. At 0730 hrs I identified a Hussar convoy, which picked me up and took me back to their HQ. I rejoined my unit at 1800 hrs that day.'

The Gladiators and solitary Lysander had encountered seven Ba.65s of 159ª *Squadriglia*, 12° *Gruppo Assalto* of 50° *Stormo*, escorted by CR.32s of 160ª *Squadriglia*. Wykeham-Barnes, flying Gladiator I L8009, had quickly despatched a single Ba.65, which became No 80 Sqn's first kill of World War 2. Moments later, however, his wingman, Sgt Kenneth Rew, was shot down and killed by the CR.32 formation leader, Capitano Duilio Fanali. Wykeham-Barnes then engaged the Fiat fighters and claimed one shot down, before falling victim to Maresciallo Romolo Cantelli.

PILOT BIOGRAPHY – PETER WYKEHAM-BARNES

Peter Wykeham-Barnes was born on 13 September 1915 at Sandhurst in Surrey, and he joined the RAF as a Halton apprentice in 1932. He was then selected to become a Cadet at the RAF College, Cranwell, and graduated in 1937. Wykeham-Barnes was posted to No 80 Sqn, and moved with the unit to Egypt in 1938. Later that year he was detached to Palestine, where he saw action against Arab dissidents, for which he received a Certificate of Distinguished Conduct.

When war began in Egypt in June 1940, Wykeham-Barnes flew the only Hurricane (P2639) in North Africa forward to Mersa Matruh on attachment to No 33 Sqn. Flying P2639 on a patrol near Sollum with four No 33 Sqn Gladiators, he engaged a formation of nine Fiat CR.42s and quickly shot down the leader with a short burst at full deflection while the Italian pilot was performing a vertical turn. In the fierce fight which ensued, Wykeham-Barnes hit a second, which was also confirmed – the first of his 17 kills, three of which were shared. On returning to No 80 Sqn, he resumed flying the Gladiator, gaining two more victories on 4 August, when he himself was obliged to bail out. Engaging the Italians once again four days later, he brought down yet another CR.42 with his Gladiator, and in the process become an ace.

Soon afterwards Wykeham-Barnes became a founder member of No 274 Sqn, formed as the first all-Hurricane unit in Egypt – he made his first claims with the squadron on 9 December. Shortly before leaving No 80 Sqn, he had become the first fighter pilot in North Africa to receive a DFC. Wykeham-Barnes continued to claim regularly throughout the desert fighting, and in April 1941 he assumed command of No 73 Sqn, with whom he made his final claims in the Hurricane. Receiving a Bar to his DFC in August, he became Wing Commander Fighters, Western Desert, in November, until being rested and then sent to the USA as an air-fighting instructor.

Wykeham-Barnes later commanded No 257 Sqn when it converted, from Hurricanes to Typhoons, and in 1942 took over No 23 Sqn – flying Mosquito II intruders – which he led to Malta, where he gained his final victories. After staff tours in the UK, he joined the 2nd Tactical Air Force, commanding a Mosquito Wing with distinction.

Wykeham-Barnes remained in the RAF post-war, serving with the Central Fighter Establishment and on exchange with the USAF during the Korean War, where he flew B-26 Invaders in combat. Returning to the UK, he commanded several jet fighter stations and filled staff appointments, all the while being regularly promoted. Head of the Far East Air Force from 1964 to 1967, his final appointment was as Deputy Chief of Air Staff. Peter Wykeham-Barnes passed away in 1995.

SPECIFICATION

TYPE: single-engined biplane fighter

ACCOMMODATION: pilot

DIMENSIONS: length 27 ft 5 in (8.36 m)
wingspan 32 ft 3 in (9.83 m)
height 10 ft 4 in (3.15 m)

WEIGHTS: empty 3450 lb (1565 kg)
maximum take-off 4750 lb (2155 kg)

PERFORMANCE: maximum speed 253 mph (407 kmh)
range 428 miles (689 km)
powerplant Bristol Mercury VIIIA/AS or IX
output 840 hp (626 kW)

ARMAMENT: four BSA Colt Browning 0.303-in machine guns on the sides of the forward fuselage and under the wings

FIRST FLIGHT DATE: 12 September 1934

OPERATORS: Belgium, China, Egypt, Eire, Finland, Greece, Iraq, Latvia, Lithuania, Norway, Portugal, South Africa, Sweden, UK

PRODUCTION: 768

The ultimate (and final) British biplane fighter of them all, the Gladiator started life as a company private venture, Gloster basing its new SS.37 (as the Gladiator was designated) very much on its predecessor, the Gauntlet. Although equipped with four guns, the design still embraced the 'old' technology of doped fabric over its wood and metal ribbed and stringered fuselage and wings. Following its first flight in September 1934, the Gladiator I was swiftly put into production, with Gloster eventually building 231 examples. It made its service debut in January 1937, and went on to fly with 26 RAF fighter squadrons. The later Mk II was fitted with the Bristol Mercury VIIIA engine, and 252 new-build machines were delivered – a number of Mk Is were also upgraded to this specification through the fitment of the later powerplant. Sixty arrestor-hooked Sea Gladiators were also built for the Royal Navy, plus a further 165 Mk I/IIs for foreign export customers. A considerable number of Gladiators were still in service when war broke out in September 1939, and although obsolete, they gave a good account of themselves in North Africa, the Middle East, over Malta and in East Africa.

Gladiator I L8009 of Flg Off Peter Wykeham-Barnes, No 80 Sqn, Sidi Barrani, Egypt, August 1940
Wykeham-Barnes attacked and shot down a Ba.65 of 159º *Squadrigilia* on 4 August 1940 to claim No 80 Sqn's first victory of World War 2.

FLYING TIGERS

'Dupouy pulled up to the left. In doing so, his right wing clipped the other wingman's ship right at the wing root, and the Jap spun into the Gulf too.'

On Christmas Day 1941, more than 150 fighters and bombers of the Japanese Imperial Army Air Force attacked Rangoon and nearby Allied installations. Opposing them were 13 Tomahawks of the American Volunteer Group's Third ('Hell's Angels') Pursuit Squadron and 14 Brewster Buffaloes of the Royal Air Force's No 67 Sqn. Ex-Army Air Corps pilot Bill Reed scrambled with his Tomahawk flight at 1115 hrs, and duly orbited uneventfully for 30 minutes before finally intercepting the enemy. After skirmishing with the escorting fighters and making a head-on pass on the bombers, which were by then returning to base, he joined his Flight Leader Parker Dupouy in a dogfight with three Nakajima Ki-43 fighters. Unable to get into a good position from which to open fire, both men dove out to escape the more manoeuvrable Japanese aeroplanes. Reed later wrote in his diary;

'By now we were 140-150 miles across the gulf from Rangoon. We started back across the Gulf at 17,000 ft, and had only gone about 30 miles out off the shore of Moulmein when we spotted three Model 0s (Ki-43s) in a V-formation below us, apparently headed home. We dropped down on their tails and surprised them. Dupouy was following me as I picked out the right-hand

Third Squadron Flight Leader William Reed stands next to his assigned Tomahawk '75' at Toungoo on 9 December 1941. Bill Reed was already flying P-40s with the Army Air Corps when he joined the AVG. He was involved in virtually all of the Third Squadron's major engagements, beginning with the battles over Rangoon on 23 and 25 December 1941 (*via Terrill Clements*)

Iain Wyllie

62 • OF THE ACES – LEGENDS OF THE SKIES

wingman. I fired from about 50 yards and Dupouy fired from
behind me and to the right. The Jap exploded right in my face.
I pulled sharply up to the right to avoid hitting him, and Dupouy
pulled up to the left. In doing so, his right wing clipped the other
wingman's ship right at the wing root and the Jap spun into the
Gulf too. The leader got the drop on me as I went by him, and
after managing to meet him almost head-on in one turn, and
losing ground in the next, I dove away. I climbed back to get at
him again, but no one was to be seen. I was damn low on gas, so
I decided to head straight over the Gulf towards Rangoon.'

Reed landed at about 1430 hrs, finding that both the airfield
and Rangoon had suffered heavy damage. Dupouy reported that
'four feet of my right wing and one half of my right aileron were
knocked off, however my aeroplane flew for three-quarters of an
hour' before he successfully dodged the bomb craters while
landing at Mingaladon at 140 mph. Reed and Dupouy's victims
were Sgt Shigekatsu Wakayama and Lt Hiroshi Okuyama of the
64th *Sentai*. The AVG lost two aircraft that day, not including
Dupouy's badly damaged fighter, while No 67 Sqn had four
Buffaloes shot down and four pilots killed. The Allies had claimed
25 Japanese aircraft destroyed during what had been the largest
aerial battle of the Pacific War up to that time.

Third Pursuit Squadron Flight Leader Parker Dupouy explains how he downed a Ki-43 with his wingtip (note the damage to his fighter) over Rangoon on Christmas Day 1941. He gave the following matter-of-fact account in his combat report. 'We turned and dove down on their tails. At point blank range – about 30 yards – we both shot at the right wingman Model "0" and his engine immediately caught fire and he dove into the ocean. I pulled up to the left, and in so doing hit the left wingman Model "0" at the left wing root near the fuselage' (*via Terrill Clements*)

Flight Leader Bill Reed pops his ears before taking off in Tomahawk '74' from Kunming in early 1942. Note the faint remains of the number under the cockpit (*via Terrill Clements*)

PILOT BIOGRAPHY – WILLIAM REED

William N Reed was born on 8 January 1917 in Stone City, Iowa, and grew up in nearby Marion. Joining the Army Air Corps on 28 January 1940, he received basic flight training at Randolph Field and advanced flight training at Kelly Field, both in Texas. Reed was commissioned as a second lieutenant on 4 October 1940 and assigned as a flight instructor, first at Randolph Field, then at Barksdale Field, Louisiana. He instructed trainees in the Tomahawk at the latter base – the fighter he would fly in the AVG. Reed viewed this as a 'humdrum' assignment, and six months later he learned that the AVG was recruiting pilots. He resigned his commission on 3 July 1941 and joined up.

Reed sailed for Burma from San Francisco on 24 July 1941 and was assigned to the all-Army Third (or 'Hell's Angels') Squadron upon his arrival in-theatre. His first victory came on 23 December 1941 during the 'Hell's Angels'' baptism of fire over Rangoon, intercepting large formations of Ki-21 bombers. Following his eventful mission on Christmas Day, Reed and the Third Squadron were withdrawn to Kunming, where the next several months were generally much quieter. On 18 March 1942, Reed and Ken Jernstedt conducted a pre-dawn strafing raid on the Japanese bases at Mudon and Moulmein, in southeastern Burma – they shared the official credit for the destruction of 15 enemy aircraft on the ground. Reed flew 75 missions with the AVG and scored three aerial victories, as well as destroying 7.5 aircraft on the ground. He served with the AVG until the group was disbanded on 4 July 1942, then returned to the US.

Turning down a job as a test pilot with North American Aviation, Reed rejoined the USAAF in early 1943. Completing gunnery training in P-47s at Millville, New Jersey, he was posted back to China on 13 November 1943, where he was assigned to the Fourteenth Air Force's P-40N-equipped Chinese-American Composite Wing (CACW). Reed scored his first victories with the wing on 16 May 1944, which he followed up with two more kills on 19 June. His last aerial victory occurred on 27 October 1944. During 66 combat missions with the CACW, he was credited with the destruction of six Japanese aircraft in the air and an additional nine on the ground, making him the wing's top ace.

Reed was killed in action on 19 December 1944 when he attempted to bail out of P-40N 43-12313 after it ran low on fuel in bad weather following a successful train-busting mission to Pengpu. He struck the tail of his aircraft and his parachute never opened. Reed was buried in China, but his body was returned to Iowa after the war.

Hawk 81-A-2 number '75' (CAF serial P-8186) of Third Squadron Flight Leader William Reed, Kunming, China, January 1942
Bill Reed will forever be remembered as the 'assigned' pilot of this Tomahawk. The ultimate fate of the aeroplane is not yet certain, but it is likely that it was lost on 10 March 1942 when Reed and four others were forced to crash-land after they ran out of fuel near Loiwing. Like all AVG pilots, Reed actually flew many different aircraft on operations, including Tomahawk 69 (P-8115), Tomahawk 79 (P-8135), Tomahawk 74 (P-8193) and Tomahawk 59 (P-8161), to name but four.

SPECIFICATION

Curtiss P-40B/C Tomahawk

TYPE:	single-engined monoplane fighter
ACCOMMODATION:	pilot
DIMENSIONS:	length 31 ft 8.5 in (9.66 m)
	wingspan 37 ft 3.5 in (11.37 m)
	height 10 ft 7 in (3.22 m)
WEIGHTS:	empty 5812 lb (2636 kg)
	maximum take-off 8058 lb (3655 kg)
PERFORMANCE:	maximum speed 345 mph (555 kmh)
	range 1230 miles (1979 km) with external drop tank
	powerplant Allison V-1710-33
	output 1040 hp (775 kW)
ARMAMENT:	two Colt-Browning 0.50-in machine guns in the nose and two or four Colt-Browning 0.30-in machine guns in the wings
FIRST FLIGHT DATE:	14 October 1938
OPERATORS:	Australia, Canada, China, Egypt, South Africa, Turkey, UK, USA, USSR
PRODUCTION:	1703

Developed simply by replacing the Twin Wasp radial engine in Curtiss's P-36 Hawk with a supercharged Allison V-1710 inline engine, the XP-40 prototype impressed the USAAC so much that an order for 524 aircraft was placed in early 1939. This was the largest order for aircraft issued to a contractor since World War 1, and the first production aircraft flew in April 1940. A large number of P-40B/Cs (no A-models were ever built) had been delivered to the USAAC by 7 December 1941, and these initially took the fight to the Japanese, but were soon shown to be inferior to enemy fighters. Aside from USAAC use, the Curtiss design also saw much action with the RAF, which christened it the Tomahawk. Some 100 ex-British aircraft were issued to the American Volunteer Group in China and Burma at around the same time. The AVG's Tomahawks differed somewhat from the airframes being shipped to Commonwealth forces from the same production lines – a fact reflected in factory photos of cockpit detail changes captioned 'H-81-A-2 (China)'. In fact the AVG's Tomahawks were not themselves identical in all details, perhaps due to incremental changes made on production lines. They were neither true P-40Bs nor P-40Cs, although AVG personnel themselves used both designations in everyday communications. Weight and performance figures for these machines were probably close to those typically given for the P-40B model, however. Indeed, when these aeroplanes were taken over by the USAAF in July 1942, many were stencilled with P-40B data blocks.

ACE IN A DAY

'I then opened fire again at another Stuka at close range, the enemy catching fire and crashing in flames near some dispersed mechanised transport.'

During the late morning of 5 December 1941, Flt Lt Clive Caldwell, the Australian flight commander with No 250 'Sudan' Sqn, led ten Tomahawks of his squadron, along with ten more from No 112 Sqn as top cover, on a patrol towards El Adem as part of the British offensive Operation *Crusader*. At 1140 hrs some ten miles west of El Gubi, a large enemy formation of Ju 87 Stukas under escort from Bf 109s, Fiat G.50s and Macchi C.200s approached the same area. The Ju 87Bs were from I./StG 1, II./StG 2 and I./StG 3, which had been joined by Italian Ju 87R *'Picchiatelli'* from 239ª *Squadriglia Autonomo B a'T.*

Caldwell, who was flying his regular Tomahawk IIB AK498, received a radio message warning him of the enemy aircraft, which were approaching from the northwest at the same altitude as the RAF fighters. The Australian put the Tomahawk formation into an immediate climb, and in less than a minute he had spotted the enemy formation off to his right. Having ordered the No 250 Sqn aircraft to line up directly astern of him, Caldwell dived on the Stukas from their rear quarter, while No 112's Tomahawks kept their fighter escorts busy. His combat report of the mission read as follows;

Clive Caldwell was the Commonwealth's leading scorer on the Tomahawk/Kittyhawk and most successful RAAF ace of the war. He is seen here as a squadron leader while in command of No 112 Sqn in North Africa in early 1942 (*via Norman Franks*)

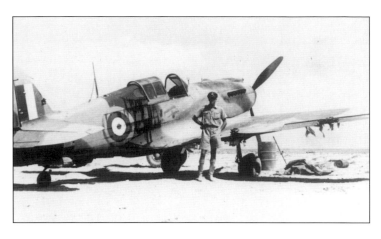

Plt Off Clive Caldwell stands by Tomahawk AK493 at Sidi Haneish on 29 August 1941 after his fighter was badly shot up by German ace Leutnant Werner Schroer. Having survived the attack, the Australian destroyed a Bf 109 on his way home! (*via Andrew Thomas*)

'I was leading the formation of two squadrons, No 112 acting as top cover to No 250 Sqn, sent to patrol a line approximately ten miles west of El Gubi, and had just reached this position at 1140 hrs when I received R/T warning that a large enemy formation was approaching from the northwest at our height. Both squadrons climbed immediately, and within a minute the enemy formation, consisting of Ju 87s with fighter escort, was sighted on our starboard side. No 250 Sqn went into line astern behind me, and as No 112 engaged the escorting fighters, we attacked the Ju 87s from the rear quarter.

'At 300 yards I opened fire with all my guns at the leader of one of the rear sections of three, allowing too little deflection, and hit

Nos 2 and 3, one of which burst into flames immediately, the other going down smoking and then bursting into flames after losing about 1000 ft. I then attacked the leader of the rear section from below and behind, opening fire with all guns at very close range. The enemy aircraft turned over and dived steeply down with the root of the starboard wing in flames. I then opened fire again at another Stuka at close range, the enemy catching fire and crashing in flames near some dispersed mechanised transport. I was then able to pull up under the belly of the one at the rear, holding the burst until very close range. The enemy aircraft dived gently straight ahead, streaming smoke, then caught fire and dived into the ground.'

Back at base, the young Australian ace, who already had nine and two shared kills to his name, was credited with five Ju 87s destroyed. It would appear that Caldwell's last two victims were the 239ª *Squadriglia 'Picchiatelli'* flown by Sottotenente Stefonia and Sergente Mangano – he was also credited with damaging a C.200.

Caldwell's brilliance as a pilot, and overall fighting qualities, were recognised with the simultaneous awarding of a DFC and Bar on 26 December after his most successful day on 5 December 1941. No other Australian airman received such a unique accolade in World War 2.

No 112 Sqn pilots pose with their CO, Sqn Ldr Clive Caldwell (extreme left), at Antelat, in Libya, in January 1942. Included in this group are fellow aces Flg Off Neville Duke (third from left, standing), Plt Off Henry Burney (to the right of Duke) and Sgt Rudy Leu (third from right, standing) (*via Andrew Thomas*)

PILOT BIOGRAPHY – CLIVE CALDWELL

Born in the Sydney suburb of Lewisham on 28 July 1911, Clive Robertson Caldwell had learned to fly with the Royal Aero Club in 1938. He joined the RAAF upon the outbreak of war and was commissioned as a pilot officer in 1940. Discovering that he was destined to become an instructor after completing his training, Caldwell resigned and reapplied as an aircrew trainee. Eventually being awarded his wings in January 1941, he was among the first RAAF-trained pilots to join Tomahawk-equipped No 250 Sqn, then based at Aqir, in Palestine, four months later.

Caldwell later recalled his thoughts on the various models of P-40 he flew;

'Of the two I preferred the Tomahawk as a pilot's aircraft, favouring only the greater lethal density of the Kittyhawk's six 0.50 calibre guns. The aeroplane handled and turned well, recovered from a spin without fuss and in general had little vice.'

Caldwell performed his first operational patrol on 14 May, and soon afterwards moved to the Western Desert, where he achieved great success during a lengthy period of intensive operations. On 26 June No 250 Sqn's Tomahawks had their first successful engagement while escorting Blenheims sent to attack Gazala. Clive Caldwell, in AK419, downed the Bf 109E flown by Leutnant Heinz Schmidt of I./JG 27 – the first of his eventual 30 victories, including three shared, which made him the leading RAAF ace of World War 2. Caldwell's aggression quickly earned him the nickname of 'Killer', something he personally detested, as fellow ace 'Bobby' Gibbes recalled;

'Clive was given the name "Killer" (which was not of his choosing, or liking) due to his habit of shooting up any enemy vehicle which he saw below when returning from a sortie. Invariably, he landed back at his base with almost no ammunition left.'

On 7 July 1941 Caldwell became the first Commonwealth pilot to claim five victories flying the P-40. After his successful tour with No 250 Sqn, he was promoted to command the elite No 112 Sqn, flying Kittyhawks, with whom he achieved further victories, before leaving for Australia via the UK. Upon returning home, Caldwell was given command of the first RAAF Spitfire wing, which he led with distinction in the defence of Darwin in 1943, and with whom he personally destroyed eight Japanese aircraft. Awarded a DSO soon afterwards, he later led a Spitfire wing in the island hopping campaign, eventually leaving the RAAF as a group captain in 1946. He then pursued a successful business career until passing away in 1994.

SPECIFICATION

Curtiss P-40B/C Tomahawk

TYPE:	single-engined monoplane fighter
ACCOMMODATION:	pilot
DIMENSIONS:	length 31 ft 8.5 in (9.66 m) wingspan 37 ft 3.5 in (11.37 m) height 10 ft 7 in (3.22 m)
WEIGHTS:	empty 5812 lb (2636 kg) maximum take-off 8058 lb (3655 kg)
PERFORMANCE:	maximum speed 345 mph (555 kmh) range 1230 miles (1979 km) with external drop tank powerplant Allison V-1710-33 output 1040 hp (775 kW)
ARMAMENT:	two Colt-Browning 0.50-in machine guns in the nose and two or four 0.30-in machine guns in the wings
FIRST FLIGHT DATE:	14 October 1938
OPERATORS:	Australia, Canada, China, Egypt, South Africa, Turkey, UK, USA, USSR
PRODUCTION:	1703

The Curtiss P-40 series of fighters was a progressive development of the company's earlier radial-engined P-36, which had been ordered in substantial numbers by the USAAC and the French *l'Armée de l'Air*. There was clearly development potential in the airframe, and this duly led to the production of a variant fitted with an Allison inline engine. France contracted for the type as the Hawk H-81, which the US designated the P-40. The British Purchasing Commission also issued an initial contract for the fighter, which was named Tomahawk in RAF service after the war axe used by the North American Indians. Trials showed that the Tomahawk would be unsuitable for service in the fighter role over Europe, and indeed the early Mk Is were woefully armed. However, it was decided that the better armed Mk IIBs should re-equip fighter squadrons in the Middle East, this decision following the December 1940 rejection of the Tomahawk by Fighter Command after the latter had conducted brief trials with several Mk IIAs. Later fitted with more powerful engines and increased armament, the aircraft, from the P-40D series onwards, was known as the Kittyhawk. As such, it was to see widespread and distinguished service with the Commonwealth air forces in many theatres, ranging from the blazing heat of North Africa to the steamy jungles of New Guinea and the Solomons. Initially, the Curtiss machine was used in the fighter role, but later it served to great effect as a fighter-bomber until war's end. Almost 50 pilots from the Commonwealth air forces claimed five or more victories flying it, and nearly 40 more aces made at least part of their 'score' on the type.

Tomahawk IIB AK498 of Flt Lt Clive Caldwell, No 250 Sqn, LG 123 Maddelena No 3, Libya, November-December 1941

Clive Caldwell of No 250 Sqn became the first Commonwealth ace to claim five victories on the Tomahawk, achieving this feat on 7 July. In November he was assigned this aircraft, which carried his 'scoreboard'. On 23 November he used AK498 to destroy two Bf 109s, but his outstanding feat with it came on 5 December when he was credited with downing five Ju 87s. His ninth, and final, confirmed claim with AK498 was on 20 December, when another Bf 109 fell to him. On Christmas Eve Caldwell also used this machine to damage the Bf 109F of 69-victory *experte* Oberleutnant Erbo Graf von Kageneck of III./JG 27, who later died of his wounds. AK498 was also used by future ace Plt Off John Waddy to make his first confirmed claim on 9 December. This aircraft was struck off charge on 1 April 1944.

BURMA
BATTLER

'We came down in a steep right-hand spiral and selected one enemy aircraft each. I got two steady bursts into mine.'

Among the units sent to reinforce the meagre RAF resources in Burma after the outbreak of war in the region in December 1941 was No 135 Sqn. The unit was commanded by one of the RAF's leading fighter pilots, Sqn Ldr Frank Carey, and initially flew aircraft borrowed from other squadrons. By late January, however, it was established at Mingaladon for the defence of the Burmese capital, Rangoon. Among its many untried pilots was 27-year-old former school teacher Plt Off Jack Storey from Australia, who made his first claim on the 29th during his first combat sortie;

'I saw three enemy aircraft behind one P-40, which was easily being out-turned. We came down in a steep right-hand spiral and selected one enemy aircraft each. I got two steady bursts into mine – hits were observed and it slipped off into the cloud to the left. Our groundcrews saw an enemy fighter dive out of the cloud and crash near a Blenheim.'

The Japanese were regularly raiding Rangoon, and the nearby airfield at Mingaladon. Just before 0900 hrs on Friday, 6 February 1942, a raid was detected and some Tomahawks from the American Volunteer Group, together with six No 135 Sqn

One of the most successful pilots of the Burma campaign was Plt Off Jack Storey, who claimed his first victory on his first operational sortie (*via Andrew Thomas*)

Two Hurricanes of No 135 Sqn are refuelled at Mingaladon in early 1942. On the right is Z5659/WK-C, which was flown by Plt Off Jack Storey in a successful combat over Mingaladon on 6 February. He also flew it on the 23rd of that month when he destroyed a 'Nate' for his fourth victory (via Andrew Thomas)

Hurricanes, scrambled to intercept. With Carey's aircraft unserviceable on the ground, it was Storey (flying Z5659/WK-C), with Sgt Roberson as his wingman, who led the squadron into battle. As the Hurricanes climbed rapidly into the sun, ground control told the pilots that the enemy were very high and in great numbers, but gave no directions! Passing through 16,000 ft, Storey sighted the Japanese aircraft off to his left, some 5000 ft above him. The enemy formation comprised 25 highly-manoeuvrable Ki-27 'Nate' (Army Type 97) fighters of the veteran 50th and 77th Sentais.

Storey had previously noted that, 'In spite of their inferior armament, the Japanese were well trained in deflection shooting. Our aircraft would sometimes come back with holes all over them. That's difficult to do.'

Having lost two fighters in the climb, Storey turned the remaining four Hurricanes to the right to get 'up-sun'. Spotting three of the enemy machines slightly above him attempting to bounce the RAF fighters, he immediately entered a left-hand vertical spiral turn. When 'up-sun', Storey fired a burst into one of the 'Nates'. A whirling free-for-all then ensued, and the Australian soon gained a good position behind one of the Japanese fighters. With a devastating burst of fire, Storey sent it spiralling down to its destruction south of Zayatkwin airfield, northeast of Rangoon.

As the slower-climbing AVG Tomahawks arrived, the Australian was engaged from behind by two more Ki-27s. Again Storey spiralled left. Ramming his throttle open, he once more swept 'up-sun', before swooping on them. He made a quarter attack on the rearmost 'Nate', firing two accurate bursts. It spun to the right and crashed. Storey was then engaged by several more Japanese fighters, but he evaded them. Although his engine was overheating by this point, he fired on two more 'Nates', which he believed he had hit, although he did not observe the results.

His ammunition exhausted, Storey managed to disengage and recover to base. There, just one bullet hole was discovered in his wing – although his spark plugs needed changing! In this epic fight against the odds, Jack Storey was credited with two Ki-27s destroyed and two probables from total RAF claims of three confirmed, three probables and three damaged. Lt Kitamura of the 77th Sentai was possibly one of his victims, for he was listed as missing by the Japanese.

The young Australian was establishing a reputation, and he eventually became the second highest scoring Commonwealth RAF pilot in Burma. Soon after this action had taken place, Storey's new CO, Sqn Ldr Barry Sutton, promoted him to flight commander, and gave him the following endorsement;

'I should feel gratified that this young Australian has got the chance to show his full worth not only as a pilot of exceptional ability, but as one of the best leaders of a formation I have ever seen'.

No mean praise from a pilot with 4.5 kills to his name, but his comments proved to be remarkably prescient.

Storey's first victim was this Nakajima Ki-27 of the 77th Sentai, which dived into the ground near a parked Blenheim at Mingaladon on 29 January 1942 (via Andrew Thomas)

PILOT BIOGRAPHY – WILLIAM STOREY

William Storey, usually known as 'Jack', was born in Victoria, Australia, on 15 November 1915. Commencing his teaching career in 1935, he volunteered for the RAAF without hesitation upon the outbreak of war. Sent to Canada to earn his wings, Storey completed his training in England and then joined No 135 Sqn in September 1941. The unit was posted to Burma shortly afterwards. Storey made his first claim following his first operational sortie, and by the end of February he had four confirmed and two probables to his name, and had been promoted to flight commander. By the time the retreat from Burma ended, he had flown over 60 hours on operations in the most desperate conditions in less than a month.

Jack Storey remained with No 135 Sqn as it rebuilt, and in early 1943 he took part in offensive sweeps down the Arakan Peninsula toward Akyab. During the morning of 5 March 1943, he led a patrol over the Japanese-held port at 21,000 ft, engaging the enemy as he later recalled;

'The Japs split up and during the dogfight, which soon took us down to 12,000 ft, more appeared and joined in. After much tail chasing I finally got an opening and carried out a downward quarter attack on a straggler and got in a beautiful deflection shot – saw de Wilde strikes on the port mainplane, engine, cockpit and tailplane. It rolled over and went straight down through clouds, streaming petrol vapour from the port wing tank. "Hawk" (Flt Lt Lee Hawkins – author) went down immediately afterwards with three Japs on his tail and said he saw the tail unit of my "Oscar" sticking up out of the water with black smoke coming up from around it.'

Storey then led his men back to the landing ground at Ritz, where his fifth victory was confirmed. After refuelling, 'A' Flight returned to Akyab, where Storey found that they were well positioned to jump a vic of 'Oscars';

'I chose the No 3 and sent him down with quite a short burst from dead astern. He plummeted down, exploding on impact on the northern tip of Baronga Island. I then singled out one lone fighter, which seemed to be looking for trouble at 2000 ft below everything. After taking a good look to ensure no trap existed, I went down after him and got in a very satisfactory burst which caused many pieces to fly off the aircraft. After pulling steeply upwards, I rolled over and was astonished to see the pilot bail out, as this was the first occasion I had actually seen a Jap do this.'

Storey was awarded the DFC on 9 April 1943. In early May he claimed his eighth, and last, victory, and soon afterwards was posted to an instructional job. He was repatriated to Australia in 1944, where he undertook further instructional work until his demobilisation after the war. Storey then completed his degree and returned to teaching until his retirement.

Hurricane IIB Z5659/WK-C of Plt Off William J Storey, No 135 Sqn, Mingaladon, Burma, February 1942
On 6 February 1942 the Japanese attacked Mingaladon airfield, on the outskirts of Rangoon, and Jack Storey scrambled in this aircraft, leading six others aloft. Three Ki-27 'Nate' fighters of the 77th Sentai jumped them, and in the subsequent fight Storey shot down two and claimed two probables. He was again flying Z5659 on 23 February when he sent a 'Nate' into the jungle in flames for his fourth victory. Storey's faithful Hurricane was eventually struck off charge on 7 July 1943.

SPECIFICATION

Hawker Hurricane
(all dimensions and performance data for the machine gun-armed Hurricane Mk II)

TYPE:	single-engined monoplane fighter
ACCOMMODATION:	pilot
DIMENSIONS:	length 32 ft 3 in (9.83 m) wingspan 40 ft 0 in (12.19 m) height 13 ft 3 in (4.04 m)
WEIGHTS:	empty 5658 lb (2566 kg) maximum take-off 7490 lb (3397 kg)
PERFORMANCE:	maximum speed 324 mph (521 kmh) range 460 miles (740 km) powerplant Rolls-Royce Merlin 24 output 1620 hp (1193 kW)
ARMAMENT:	eight Browning 0.303-in machine guns in wings
FIRST FLIGHT DATE:	11 June 1940
OPERATORS:	Australia, Belgium, Canada, Eire, Finland, France, India, The Netherlands, Portugal, South Africa, UK, USSR, Yugoslavia
PRODUCTION:	8406

On 11 June 1940 a Hurricane Mk I airframe was flown with a two-stage supercharged Merlin XX engine fitted in place of the Merlin III. Designated the Hurricane Mk II, deliveries of the machine to frontline units commenced in September of that year. The first Series 1 Mk IIs retained the standard wings of the Hurricane Mk I, but the Series 2 machines boasted fuselage strengthening to allow the fitment of wings featuring universal attachment points for external stores. An extra fuselage bay was also incorporated into the machine, increasing the fighter's overall length by seven inches. The 12-gun Mk IIB was produced from late 1940, and the following year the four 20 mm cannon Mk IIC also made its service debut. All Mk II variants had underwing attachments for bombs, rockets, drop tanks and other external stores. Although deemed obsolescent for the day fighter role in the UK, the Hurricane II continued to serve as a fighter-bomber and night intruder on the Channel Coast into 1943. In North Africa, the Mediterranean and the Far East, the Hurricane was the most modern fighter available to the RAF. The aircraft, in its Sea Hurricane guise, was also the primary carrier-based fighter in service with the Fleet Air Arm in 1941-42. Although Hurricane production finally ceased in September 1944, the aircraft remained in frontline service in the Far East until VJ-Day.

NIP'S NEMESIS

'They left me off the mission yesterday. Shit on it, I'm going in.'

This official USAAF photograph of then 2Lt Donald 'Fibber' McGee was taken at Seven-Mile Strip shortly after he had claimed his three kills in May 1942 (*via John Stanaway*)

The Airacobras of the 8th Fighter Group's 35th and 36th Fighter Squadrons performed their first interception over Port Moresby on 1 May 1942. One of the pilots involved in this engagement was future ace 1Lt Don 'Fibber' McGee, who was told to perform airfield cover while two other sections of P-39s went looking for the Japanese aircraft that Allied spotters had radioed were heading for Port Moresby. However, once airborne, the American pilots failed to find any trace of Japanese aerial activity.

McGee had taken off on his own when his wingman's P-39 suffered mechanical trouble and refused to start. After two hours of uneventful patrolling, he was instructed to land since all the P-39s were now low on fuel. Having just let down to 3500 ft, McGee heard his ground controller, 'Golden Voice', call out a warning that Zeros were attacking the airfield at that very moment. The P-39 pilot could see nothing in the immediate vicinity, and he looked at his fuel gauge and gulped when he realised that there was less than 20 gallons remaining in his tank – enough for just nine minutes of combat. At that moment he spotted a single Zero making a run across the revetment area of his base at Seven-Mile Strip.

The debate flashed through his mind – he would be going into the fight with no gas, and he was low and had insufficient airspeed. The Zero then turned in to make another pass and McGee realised that he had the advantage of surprise. He had also missed out on the P-39's baptism of fire in-theatre the previous day, which still rankled with him. 'They left me off the mission yesterday. Shit on it, I'm going in', he thought to himself.

McGee retarded power to conserve fuel and bit down anxiously on his lip when he realised that he was closing much too slowly. He watched the Zero (flown by Petty Officer 1st Class Yoshisuke Arita of the Tainan *Kokutai*) lining up behind a P-39 that was taking off just at that moment, and he wondered which line on the gunsight he should use to ensure hits on the enemy aeroplane. One burst went off to the right and a second sailed under the unsuspecting Japanese pilot. McGee then corrected his aim and saw tracers strike all over the Zero. It rolled over to the right and started an inverted dive into the jungle below. McGee was about to follow when he realised that he was only 150 ft above the ground. He passed the Zero as it struck the tree canopy and looked back to see his target explode when it hit the ground.

McGee then found himself surrounded by 'a mass of red balls', which forced him to skid and jink in order to avoid 'the horrible blinking guns on the wings of the Zero'. Somehow he avoided being killed until the last Zero had departed for home. The P-39 pilot stayed low over the water of Bootless Inlet, some three miles southwest of Seven-Mile Strip. When McGee finally landed, he almost immediately ran out of fuel. Some of the groundcrewmen who rushed out to greet the pilot pointed at McGee's P-39F, and he obliged by holding up one finger to signify the 36th FS's first aerial victory. Their pointing had nothing to do with McGee's kill,

2Lt Donald 'Fibber' McGee poses with his groundcrew at Seven-Mile Strip sometime after claiming his final P-39 kills on 29 May 1942. He is adamant that he scored five aerial victories with the Airacobra, despite official USAF records crediting him with just three confirmed kills and one probable victory (*via John Stanaway*)

however, as the groundcrew were showing their amazement at the two 20 mm shell hits in the fighter's tail, the numerous machine gun bullet holes in the wings and the shrapnel marks in the horizontal stabiliser and elevators. McGee then looked up and saw the bullet hole through the back of the canopy from a round that had shattered the sunglasses on his head without harming him!

McGee's kill was confirmed when the wreckage of the Zero was found only about a mile away from the airstrip. It was the first victory for the 36th FS, and marked quite an auspicious beginning for such grim business.

Don McGee's P-39D-1 42-38338 *Nip's Nemesis II* was highly unusual in that it carried identical artwork and kill tallies on both sides of the fuselage – groundcrews were usually hard-pressed to find the time to decorate one side of an operational aeroplane, let along both of them! The artwork on the doors of this machine shows a Japanese fighter being grabbed by a God-like hand. 'Fibber' McGee would claim a further two kills flying P-38s with the 80th FS during the course of 1943, before going on to score his final victory in a P-51D over Germany while commanding the 357th FG's 363rd FS in March 1945 (*via John Stanaway*)

PILOT BIOGRAPHY – DONALD McGEE

Born in Brooklyn, New York, on 15 July 1920, Donald Charles McGee enlisted in the Army on 1 July 1939 and served in the infantry prior to becoming an aviation cadet on 30 April 1941. Undergoing training at Craig Field, Alabama, he was commissioned as a second lieutenant and rated a pilot on 12 December 1941. McGee joined the 36th Pursuit Squadron of the 8th Pursuit Group nine days later, the unit flying P-39Ds in defence of New York from nearby Mitchel Field.

Shipped out with the rest of the group to help defend Australia, McGee arrived in Brisbane in early March 1942. In late April the 8th PG was posted north to Seven-Mile Strip on the outskirts of the New Guinean capital, Port Moresby. The Japanese were planning a major offensive aimed at ejecting the Allies from New Guinea, and the three P-39 squadrons that made up the 8th would play a key part in defending Port Moresby.

Donald McGee had a dream start to his combat career, downing one of nine Zeros that he engaged on his first mission on 1 May 1942 – this was also the first of 453 victories that would be credited to the now redesignated 8th Fighter Group (FG) by war's end. He added two more Zeros to his tally on 29 May, bouncing the fighters from above some 50 miles southeast of Port Moresby.

Transferring to the P-38-equipped 80th FS towards the end of 1942, McGee claimed his fourth victory on 12 April 1943 when he destroyed a 'Betty' bomber heading for Port Moresby. His all-important fifth kill came over Wewak on 15 September when he downed a 'Tony' fighter. Two months later McGee, now a captain, returned home after completing his 154-mission tour. Spending the next nine months instructing tyro fighter pilots on the P-47, McGee succeeded in getting back into combat with a posting to the Eighth Air Force's P-51D-equipped 363rd FS/357th FG, based in England. Arriving in the late summer, he eventually became CO of the 363rd, and then the 364th FS. McGee scored his final aerial kill on 2 March 1945 in a 363rd FS P-51D when he downed a Bf 109 near Magdeburg, in Germany.

Remaining in the air force post-war, he was promoted to lieutenant colonel on 1 June 1952 and eventually retired from the USAF in October 1967.

P-39D-1 41-38338 *Nip's Nemesis II* of 2Lt Don C McGee, 36th FS/8th FG, Port Moresby, New Guinea, June 1942

One of the few P-39 pilots to have more than one victory confirmed during the 8th FG's initial combat deployment to New Guinea, 'Fibber' McGee still maintains that he downed at least five aircraft with the Airacobra in 1942. One of those unconfirmed kills was officially recorded as a probable (a Zero attacked on 5 May near Port Moresby), while another unspecified engagement saw McGee credited with having damaged a Japanese aircraft. In any event, his single Zero kill on 1 May, followed by a pair of Mitsubishi fighters 28 days later, were officially recognised. It remains unclear whether McGee scored any of his victories with this particular P-39, which was assigned to him after the original *Nip's Nemesis* was damaged beyond repair during the engagement of 1 May.

SPECIFICATION

Bell P-39D Airacobra

TYPE:	single-engined monoplane fighter
ACCOMMODATION:	pilot
DIMENSIONS:	length 30 ft 2 in (9.19 m) wingspan 34 ft 0 in (10.36 m) height 11 ft 10 in (3.61 m)
WEIGHTS:	empty 5645 lb (2560 kg) maximum take-off 8300 lb (3765 kg)
PERFORMANCE:	maximum speed 386 mph (621 kmh) range 650 miles (1046 km) powerplant Allison V-1710-85 output 1200 hp (895 kW)
ARMAMENT:	one American Armament Corporation T-9 37 mm cannon and two Colt-Browning 0.50-in machine guns in the nose, two or four Colt-Browning 0.30-in machine guns in the wings and one 500-lb (227 kg) bomb on an external rack
FIRST FLIGHT DATE:	6 April 1938 (XP-39)
OPERATORS:	France, Italy, Portugal, UK, USA, USSR
PRODUCTION:	9594

Bell's revolutionary P-39 introduced the concept of both the centrally-mounted powerplant and the tricycle undercarriage to single-engined fighters, the aircraft's unusual configuration stemming from its principal armament, the propeller hub-mounted T-9 37 mm cannon. In order to allow the weapon to be housed in the nose the P-39's engine was moved aft to sit virtually over the rear half of the wing centre-section. This drastically shifted the aircraft's centre of gravity, thus forcing designers to adopt a tricycle undercarriage. Unfortunately, the P-39's radical design was not matched by stunning performance figures particularly at heights exceeding 14,000 ft, its normally-aspirated Allison V-1710 struggling in the 'thinner' air at these altitudes – following a service evaluation of the YP-39 in 1938-39, Bell was told by USAAC and NACA officials that a turbocharged version of the V-1710 then available for the Airacobra was not needed! Once the fighter entered service in 1941 the wisdom of this decision was quickly called into question. Indeed, so compromised was the aircraft's 'combatability' in its designated role that it was soon relegated to close air support duties in theatres where other aircraft could be employed as fighters. Operating at much lower altitudes over the eastern front, the Soviet air force did, however, achieve great aerial success with the Bell fighter, utilising some 5000 from 1942 onwards.

ITALIAN 'THUNDER-BOLT'

'His nose filled three-quarters of my gunsight, and it was easy to hit him after a short deflection shot to correct my fire.'

On 19 August 1942, Tenente Pilota Giulio Reiner was ordered to take-off in his Macchi C.202 Folgore from his base at Fuka, not far from El Alamein, with seven other fighters (four from 73ª *Squadriglia* and four from 96ª *Squadriglia*) to intercept enemy aircraft which had been identified over the frontline by German Freya radar. Reiner's wingman on this occasion was Tenente Pilota Gibellini, who was undertaking his first combat sortie.

Arriving over El Hamman at a height of 6000 metres, the formation spotted some 20 Hurricanes below them carrying out strafing attacks. While diving down to intercept the fighter-bombers, Reiner noticed ten Spitfires 1000 metres above his left wing, which were escorting the Hurricanes. They immediately turned towards the Italian formation once the latter aircraft started to dive. Reiner (followed by his flight) quickly steepened his dive, before throwing his fighter into a tight banking left turn. As a result of this high-g manoeuvre, he could now see the underside of one of the Spitfires.

'His nose filled three-quarters of my gunsight', Reiner later recalled, 'and it was easy to hit him after a short deflection shot to correct my fire'. The Spitfire was mortally damaged by the weight of the Italian pilot's fire, giving Reiner his third victory – and his

Tenente Giulio Reiner is seen at Gorizia in August 1941 while serving as a test pilot with the *Centro Sperimentale* (Experimental Test Centre). Note that his flying jacket bears the 'Gamba di Ferro' insignia of his previous unit, 73ª *Squadriglia*, 9° *Gruppo*, 4° *Stormo* (*via Giorgio Apostolo*)

Tenente Giulio Reiner, commander of 73ª *Squadriglia* (9° *Gruppo*, 4° *Stormo*), poses for an official photograph alongside his C.202 at Castelbenito in early January 1943 (*via Giorgio Apostolo*)

first success in the C.202. But the fight did not end there, for the inexperienced Tenente Gibellini had given chase to another Spitfire, and by so doing had lost touch with his leader. Finding himself alone, he was swiftly shot down, despite the late intervention of Reiner. Four more Spitfires then turned on the latter pilot, and he had to use every ounce of his undoubted flying skill to escape. After finally landing at Fuka, Reiner was told by his groundcrew that they had counted 107 machine gun holes in his aircraft.

His victim during this sortie was almost certainly future ten-kill Spitfire ace Plt Off C J 'Sammy' Samouelle of No 92 Sqn, who successfully crash-landed his badly-damaged Spitfire Mk VC trop (BR523) behind the Allied frontline.

As this engagement had proven, the C.202 was a good match for the Spitfire Mk V, being a vast improvement on previous Italian fighters types like the Macchi C.200 and Fiat CR.42 and G.50. Nevertheless, a well-trained RAF fighter pilot still felt confident when taking on an opponent flying a Folgore, as leading Allied ace in the Mediterranean Neville Duke explained;

'We felt we had the measure of the Italian fighters, especially the C.200s, G.50s and CR.42s that we encountered in the early stages of the North African campaign. The Italian pilots were much more inclined to engage in dogfights than the Germans, but the lower performance and greater manoeuvrability of their aircraft accounted for this. They were certainly very fine aerobatic pilots, but seemed to enter combat more in the spirit of a medieval joust than of a life and death struggle. They also appeared to have problems with inter-aircraft communication in the air, and were consequently easier to bounce.'

Tenente Giulio Reiner's Macchi C.202 73-4 was photographed in this rare colour shot taken at Fuka, on the Egyptian coast, in August 1942 (*via Giorgio Apostolo*)

PILOT BIOGRAPHY – GIULIO REINER

Giulio Reiner was born in Como on 12 April 1915. A conscientious student and an enthusiastic athlete, by the time he obtained his diploma in 1935 he was already in possession of a private pilot's licence from the Como Aero Club. He then volunteered to join the *Regia Aeronautica* as a temporary officer, and on completing his training was assigned to 199ª *Squadriglia Bombardamento Marittimo* (Maritime Bomber Squadron), flying Savoia S.55 flying boats.

In July 1939 he joined Fiat CR.42-equipped 73ª *Squadriglia*, 9° *Gruppo*, 4° *Stormo*, and at the end of June 1940 he moved with the unit to Sicily to participate in the opening raids on Malta. The following month the *stormo* was transferred to North Africa, where Reiner scored his first two kills. The first of these successes was claimed during a routine armed reconnaissance patrol along the Allied frontline on the evening of 12 October 1940, Reiner accompanying his *gruppo* commander, Maggiore Ernesto Botto. Having completed an uneventful patrol, the two pilots were approaching their El Adem base when they spotted three Blenheims preparing to bomb the airfield. They immediately attacked. Following a long and drawn out encounter, Reiner was credited with two bombers destroyed and Botto one. RAF records fail to confirm these claims, however, stating that three No 55 Sqn Blenheims returned to base with 'battle damage'.

The *stormo* was sent back to Italy on Christmas Day 1940 in order to commence its re-equipment with Macchi C.200s. Prior to Reiner seeing further action, he was transferred to the *Centro Sperimentale* (Experimental Test Centre) at Guidonia, where new prototypes were tested. Remaining there for over a year, he was heavily involved in the shipboard catapult-launch trials of the Reggiane Re.2000 fighter.

In July 1942 Reiner returned to take command of 73ª *Squadriglia*, which had been supporting the renewed Axis campaign in North Africa since late May. During the course of his second tour he shot down seven aircraft (four Spitfires, a P-40, a Boston and a Wellington) in the space of six months. Fleeing from Tripoli in January 1943, 73ª *Squadriglia* next saw action over Sicily in June. Promoted to the rank of capitano, Reiner claimed a P-38 on 13 July, which took his tally to ten individual kills, eight probables and three destroyed on the ground.

Following the Armistice, he shared in the fortunes of 4° *Stormo* within the *Aeronautica Co-Belligerante*, seeing action in the Balkans. Eventually attaining the rank of maggiore due to his wartime service, Reiner ended the conflict with a Silver Medal for Military Valour and an Iron Cross, Second Class, with two citations for further Silver Medals being lost in the chaos following the Armistice.

Giulio Reiner, who left the service in 1949, worked as an engineer in Como and regularly flew at the local aero club until he passed away in the spring of 2003.

SPECIFICATION

Macchi C.202 Folgore

TYPE:	single-engined monoplane fighter
ACCOMMODATION:	pilot
DIMENSIONS:	length 29 ft 0.5 in (8.85 m) wingspan 34 ft 8.5 in (10.58 m) height 9 ft 11.5 in (3.03 m)
WEIGHTS:	empty 5545 lb (2515 kg) maximum take-off 6766 lb (3069 kg)
PERFORMANCE:	maximum speed 372 mph (598 kmh) range 475 miles (764 km) powerplant Alfa Romeo RA.1000 RC41-1 Monsone (Daimler-Benz DB 601A) output 1175 hp (876 kW)
ARMAMENT:	two Breda-SAFAT 12.7 mm machine guns in the nose; later aircraft had two additional Breda-SAFAT 7.7 mm machine guns in the wings, and some with two Mauser MG 151 20 mm cannon under wings; C.202CB, guns and 705-lb (320 kg) bomb load under wings
FIRST FLIGHT DATE:	10 August 1940
OPERATOR:	Italy
PRODUCTION:	approximately 1200

Macchi's C.200, which had entered service in late 1939, had been a solid, reliable, fighter for the first 18 months of World War 2. However, it had always suffered from a lack of straightline speed, and this became readily apparent as the war in the Mediterranean intensified in late 1941. To solve this problem, Macchi turned away from home-grown radial engines for the Saetta's replacement and instead chose to use Daimler-Benz's excellent DB 601A inline engine as proven in the Bf 109E. The resulting fighter was 60 mph faster than the C.200, possessed a superior rate of climb and could cruise at altitudes in excess of 37,500 ft. Designated the C.202, initial production aircraft reached the frontline in July 1941 fitted with imported German engines, but the remaining 800+ were equipped with the licence-built Alfa Romeo version. Unfortunately for frontline fighter pilots, Macchi once again restricted the aircraft's armament to just two 12.7 mm machine guns, although late-build examples were fitted with two additional underwing guns. The Folgore quickly proved superior to both the Hurricane II and P-40 Tomahawk/Kittyhawk during its first North African engagements, and examples would later see action over the Balkans, the Western Desert, Sicily, the eastern front and Malta.

C.202 Serie III MM7944 of Tenente Giulio Reiner, CO of 73ª *Squadriglia*, 9° *Gruppo*, 4° *Stormo*, Fuka, Eqypt, August 1942

This aircraft's camouflage consists of mottling applied in Nocciola Chiaro over a Verde Oliva Scuro base. Note that MM7944 has white wingtips to denote its assignment to the North African theatre. Barely visible on its fin are two kill markings.

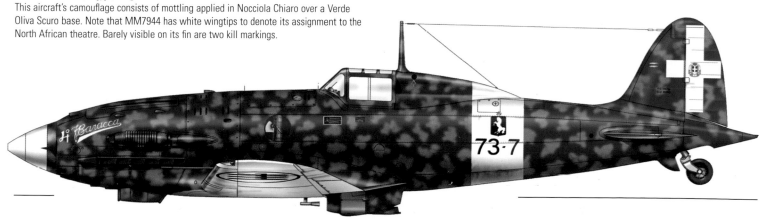

CENTURION

'He began a shallow turn to the left, which gave me the opportunity I had been waiting for. I squeezed the trigger. Wham! I had hit him with my first few rounds.'

The third-ranking Luftwaffe fighter ace of World War 2, Günther Rall scored all but three of his aerial victories on the eastern front. His achievements are all the more remarkable for the fact that he broke his back in three places when he crash-landed his damaged fighter after taking a flak hit on 28 November 1941. It would be nine months before he returned to ops and resumed command of his old *Staffel*, 8./JG 52. By that time German forces were advancing on Stalingrad. But Rall's unit was supporting the lesser-known offensive down into the Caucasus aimed at capturing that region's oil wells;

'When I crashed I had 36 kills. I returned to flying in August 1942 and was quite eager to get going again. I felt I had lost much time. Within two months I had achieved my 100th victory, and had been awarded both the Knight's Cross and the Oak Leaves.'

Rall's vivid and analytical memory means that he can recall the circumstances behind almost every kill he made – location and

Recently returned to ops nine months after breaking his back in a crash-landing, Oberleutnant Günther Rall also sports a newly-won Knight's Cross. Seen with him in front of 'Black 13' are two veteran NCOs – 'Charlie' Gratz (left) and Friedrich Wachowiak (right) – of his *Staffel*, each of whom had been similarly decorated during his enforced absence (*via John Weal*)

An example of the close links forged between pilot and groundcrew was provided by Hauptmann Günther Rall on the occasion of his double century, claimed at Makeyevka on 29 August 1943. As well as posing with fellow pilots for a commemorative snapshot, Rall – third from left – made sure that his mechanics were part of the celebrations too (*via John Weal*)

It was the accepted custom in the *Jagdwaffe* that returning pilots were greeted first by their crew chiefs. Here, Major Günther Rall gets a hearty handshake for victory number 250 (a La-5 brought down south of Zaporozhe on 28 November 1943). Only after this ritual had been observed could his fellow pilots carry Rall, shoulder-high, glass in hand, to the mess tent, where further refreshment awaited (*via John Weal*)

weather conditions, his position and movements in relation to those of his opponent, and the final outcome. He described the despatch of one Soviet fighter down in the Caucasus thus;

'I knew I had him. We were hurtling along together at ground level, me sitting on the enemy's tail and matching my speed to his. He began a shallow turn to the left, which gave me the opportunity I had been waiting for. I squeezed the trigger. Wham! I had hit him with my first few rounds. He went straight in, throwing up a tremendous shower of dirt and dust. There was nothing left but scattered debris. When he hit the ground, he had disintegrated.'

What Rall is not interested in is numbers. 'I can't talk about a particular incident and say "That was number 80 or 90 or whatever"'. But his logbook shows that his 100th kill was another Soviet fighter. It is listed there simply as a LaGG, but it is believed that his victim was, in fact, one of the new Lavochkin La-5s – a re-engined development of the earlier LaGG-3 – which had first entered service on the Stalingrad front several weeks earlier.

When Oberleutnant Günther Rall took off with his wingman, Leutnant Hans Funcke, from their forward landing ground at Soldatskaya, some 125 miles (200 km) east of Mount Elbruz – the highest peak in the Caucasus, and in all of Europe – in the early afternoon of 22 October 1942, he was just three short of his century. The pair were on a *freie Jagd*, or 'free-hunting', mission, with Rall flying his usual Bf 109G-2 'Black 1'.

Shortly after 1430 hrs they spotted two LaGGs some 4000 ft (1200 m) above the foothills of the Caucasus. Rall claimed them both in the space of a minute, Hans Funcke confirming that the two enemy machines had gone down on fire and exploded on the ground – numbers 98 and 99. Exactly three minutes later, at 1436 hrs, Rall caught a third at low-level. Another burst of fire and the Lavochkin bellied in trailing smoke to make it 100!

Seen in August 1942, soon after his return to frontline ops, Oberleutnant Günther Rall poses in front of Bf 109G-2 'Yellow 1' of 9./JG 52. Although from the same *Gruppe*, this machine was not part of his *Staffel* (*via John Weal*)

PILOT BIOGRAPHY – GÜNTHER RALL

The third of the *Jagdwaffe's* trio of 'top three' scorers – after Erich Hartmann's 352 and Gerhard Barkhorn's 301 – Günther Rall claimed 275 aircraft destroyed, all but three of them on the eastern front. Born in Gaggenau, Baden, on 10 March 1918, Rall's military career had begun as an officer-cadet with Infantry Regiment 13, and he had then transferred to the Luftwaffe. Posted to 8./JG 52 just prior to the outbreak of war, Rall achieved his first kill (a Curtiss Hawk 75) on 18 May 1940.

He was appointed *Staffelkapitän* of 8./JG 52 in July, but like Hartmann and Barkhorn, he would fail to score against the RAF, and it was not until the campaign in the east that Rall, too, came into his own. On 28 November 1941, after claiming a pair of I-16s near Rostov, he was seriously injured in a crash-landing. His back broken in three places and in a plaster cast for many months, it was late in July 1942 before he rejoined his *Staffel*. Rall claimed kill 65 on 2 September, for which he was awarded the Knight's Cross the following day. On 22 October he reached his century, and received the Oak Leaves four days later.

Assuming command of III. *Gruppe* in July 1943, Rall became the third pilot to reach the 200 mark (on 29 August 1943), which earned him the Swords, and the second to achieve 250. In April 1944, with 273 kills under his belt, he was transferred to Defence of the Reich duties as *Kommandeur* of II./JG 11. Here, he would claim just two more victories. On 12 May Rall scored his 275th, and final, kill of the war – a P-47 east of Koblenz – but he was himself severely injured during the dogfight. Made *Geschwaderkommodore* of JG 300 in early 1945, Rall spent some months as a PoW following VE-Day.

He joined the newly-formed Bundesluftwaffe in the 1950s, and was instrumental in helping to push through Germany's controversial F-104 programme – he duly led the Starfighter-equipped *JaboGeschwader* 34. After attaining the topmost rank in the Bundesluftwaffe (Chief of the Air Staff), Günther Rall's last position before retirement, in 1975, was as a member of the NATO Military Committee.

SPECIFICATION

**Messerschmitt Bf 109G/K
(all dimensions and performance data for Bf 109G-6)**

TYPE: single-engined monoplane fighter

ACCOMMODATION: pilot

DIMENSIONS: length 29 ft 7.5 in (9.03 m)
wingspan 32 ft 6.5 in (9.92 m)
height 8 ft 2.5 in (2.50 m)

WEIGHTS: empty 5893 lb (2673 kg)
maximum take-off 7496 lb (3400 kg)

PERFORMANCE: maximum speed 386 mph (621 kmh)
range 620 miles (998 km) with external tank
powerplant Daimler-Benz DB 605AM
output 1800 hp (1342 kW)

ARMAMENT: one Rheinmetall Borsig MK 108 20 mm cannon in propeller hub and two Rheinmetall Borsig MG 131 13 mm machine guns in upper cowling, two Mauser MG 151 20 mm cannon in underwing gondolas; provision for various underfuselage and underwing stores

FIRST FLIGHT DATE: late summer 1941

OPERATORS: Bulgaria, Croatia, Finland, Germany, Hungary, Italy, Rumania, Slovakia, Switzerland, Spain

PRODUCTION: approximately 24,000 G-models and around 750 K-models

The Bf 109G combined the F-model's refined airframe with the larger, heavier and considerably more powerful 1475 hp DB 605 engine to produce the most successful Messerschmitt fighter variant of them all. Cockpit pressurisation was also introduced for the first time with the G-1, although most later sub-variants lacked this feature. Produced in staggering numbers from early 1942 until war's end, more than 24,000+ Bf 109G/Ks were constructed in total – including an overwhelming 14,212 in 1944. Numerous modifications to the basic G-1 were introduced either in the factory (as *Umrüst-Bausätze* factory conversion sets) or in the field (*Rüstsätze*), and these included provision for extra armament, additional radios, introduction of a wooden tailplane, the fitting of a lengthened tailwheel and the installation of the MW50 water/menthanol-boosted DB 605D engine. In an attempt to standardise the equipment of the frontline force, Messerschmitt produced the Bf 109G-6 in late 1942, and this model included many of these previously ad hoc additions. Unfortunately, the continual addition of weighty items like wing cannon and larger engines to the once slight airframe of the Bf 109 eliminated much of the fighter's manoeuvrability, and instead served to emphasise the aircraft's poor low speed performance, lateral control and ground handling. The final variant to enter widespread service with the Luftwaffe was the Bf 109K-4.

Bf 109G-2 'Black 13' of Oberleutnant Günther Rall, *Staffelkapitän* 8./JG 52, Gostanovka, Russia, August 1942

Oberleutnant Günther Rall flew 'Black 13' upon his return to the command of 8. *Staffel* on 28 August 1942, exactly nine months to the day after being severely wounded the previous November. At that time he had claimed just 36 kills. He would add 235 more Soviet victories to his score (latterly as *Kommandeur* of III./JG 52) before his transfer to the west in the spring of 1944. Note III. *Gruppe's* 'Barbed cross' badge forward of the windshield and the wavy bar symbol on the aft fuselage. This particular machine has long been associated with Günther Rall, although he flew it only occasionally. His usual mount at this time, in accordance with his position as *Staffelkapitän*, was 'Black 1'.

CAUCASUS CLASH

'The Slovaks revelled in the performance of their Bf 109Es, even if the aircraft had already seen extensive service with the Luftwaffe in Western Europe and North Africa.'

On the morning of 28 November 1942, members of 13(*slow*)./JG 52 encountered Soviet fighters for the first time. During a *freie Jagd* near Tuapse, in the Caucasus, two Slovak Bf 109E-7s, piloted by porucik (second lieutenant) Vladimir Krisko and catnik (sergeant) Jozef Jancovic, met nine Soviet Polikarpov I-153 Chaika biplanes. After a short fight, three kills were claimed by the Slovaks, the first by Krisko in Bf 109E-7 Wk-Nr 6474 'White 12' and the other two by Jancovic. However, due to the rigorous German checking procedure, none of these kills was officially confirmed.

This combat was the culmination of many months of training by a handful of Slovakian pilots who had at last been given the opportunity of engaging the enemy in aircraft that gave them a fighting chance of emerging victorious. Having flown obsolete Avia B 534 biplane fighters in both the Polish campaign in September 1939 and the invasion of the USSR in June 1941, the Slovaks revelled in the performance of their Bf 109Es, even if the aircraft had already seen extensive service with the Luftwaffe in Western Europe and North Africa.

Nadporucik Vladimir Krisko was one of only three Slovakian officers to become an ace. As deputy CO of 13(*slow*)./JG 52, he claimed the destruction of nine Soviet aircraft, including four Yak-1s, two LaGG-3s and a single La-5, Il-2 and Pe-2. He commanded a readiness squadron on home defence duties and, during the uprising, a combined squadron. After the war Krisko led the 1st Air Regiment, and he was forced to leave the Czechoslovak Air Force in 1951 with the rank of major (*via Jiri Rajlich*)

On 26 February 1942, 105 Slovakian airmen, led by Maj Vladimir Kacka, left their homeland on a long train journey. The party, which included 19 fighter pilots (one of whom was Vladimir Krisko), was bound for Karup-Grøve airfield in occupied Denmark. There, German instructors were to teach them how to fly and service the Bf 109E in a unit that was designated 5(*Slowakei*). *Schul-Staffel Jagdgruppe* Drontheim. The theory section of the training course started on 3 March, and was followed by practical flying training starting on the 27th. The Slovak pilots received basic training in Arado Ar 96B training aircraft, before moving on to the Bf 109B/D and finally the *Emil*. All the students were experienced pilots, so their training progressed

MARK POSTLETHWAITE GAvA

relatively smoothly. The course culminated with firing at ground targets between 15 and 18 June, and officially ended on 1 July.

If training Slovak fighter pilots to fly the Bf 109 was relatively straightforward, the same could not be said for the acquisition of the new equipment. Instead of the 12 Bf 109E-7s that had initially been offered to the Slovaks in early 1942, two E-2s, one E-3, five E-4s and four E-7s were eventually ferried home by Slovak pilots between 1 July and 5 September. The aircraft were well-worn examples which had seen combat in France, over Britain and in North Africa. Some had been crashed and repaired several times. In any case, by that time the *Emil* had been replaced in frontline Luftwaffe service by the more modern Bf 109F. For now, though, they represented the most up-to-date equipment available to the Slovak Air Force.

Of the two pilots involved in the first *Emil* action of 28 November 1942, 'Jozo' Jancovic would claim seven confirmed victories before being fatally wounded while flying Bf 109G-2 Wk-Nr 14380 in combat with LaGG-3 fighters over the south coast of the Sea of Azov on 29 March 1943. He crash-landed near the village of Akhtanizovskaya, but died the next day. Between February and July 1943, 'Vlado' Krisko shot down nine Soviet aircraft. One year later he played an active part in the anti-Nazi uprising in Slovakia and survived the war.

Combat-weary Bf 109Es used by the Luftwaffe in Western Europe and North Africa were the first modern fighters issued to the Slovaks, who received more than 20 worn-out *Emils* from the Germans in 1942-43 (*via Jiri Rajlich*)

A pair of Slovakian Bf 109G-4/R6s prepare to taxi out at the start of yet another sortie from Anapa in April 1943. 'Yellow 1' was occasionally flown by rotnik Izidor Kovarik (28 kills) and nadporucik Vladimir Krisko (nine kills). After re-equipment with *Gustavs*, the pilots of 13(*slow*)./JG 52 were soon able to demonstrate total mastery of their new mounts. The arrival of these machines coincided with an increase in aerial combat, and the Slovakian pilots' overall tally rose rapidly. The 50th kill was gained on 21 March, the 100th on 27 April, the 150th on 20 June and the 200th on 24 September 1943 (*via Jiri Rajlich*)

PILOT BIOGRAPHY – VLADIMIR KRISKO

Vladimir Krisko was born on 19 August 1915 in Kochanovce, in Western Slovakia. After completing his schooling, he enlisted in the Czechoslovak Air Force and attended Military Flying School at Prostejov between 1933 and 1935. When Slovakia ceded from the Czech state in March 1939, forcing the disbandment of the air force, Krisko was serving as a sergeant pilot with the light bomber-equipped No 74 Sqn (a part of Air Regiment 6) at Brno, in Moravia. Following his repatriation back to the newly-created Slovakian state, he joined No 64 Sqn, based at Piestany. With the Slovakian Air Force suffering from a shortage of officers, Krisko was promoted to lieutenant (*porucik*) in August 1940 following a period of study at the Military Academy.

His first assignment to the eastern front came in the summer of 1941, when he served as an observer in Letov S-328s with No 2 Sqn. He then completed fighter training and Bf 109 conversion with 5 (*Slowakei*). *Schul-Staffel Jagdgruppe* Drontheim in occupied Denmark, and in October 1942 commenced his second tour on the eastern front. Promoted to deputy CO of 13(*slow*)./JG 52, Krisko saw extensive combat over the Caucasus, Kuban and Black Sea fronts through to July 1943 – he scored nine confirmed kills during the course of 156 combat sorties.

Returning to Slovakia, Krisko became CO of the Readiness Squadron, which was equipped with brand new Bf 109G-6s and tasked with defending the Slovak capital and the Povazi Valley industrial area. Grounded due to illness when his unit went into combat for the first time on 26 June 1944, Krisko missed the massacre which befell his squadronmates when eight of the nine Bf 109Gs that intercepted attacking USAAF bomber formations were shot down by escorting Mustangs and Lightnings from the Fifteenth Air Force.

When the anti-German Slovak National Uprising commenced on 29 August 1944, Krisko joined the Combined Squadron at Tri Duby aerodrome, in Central Slovakia, as its last CO. During the Uprising, he flew another 20 combat sorties against German forces in his country. While some insurgent airmen were evacuated to the Soviet Union, he remained in Slovakia after the collapse of the Uprising and served alongside the partisan army as it fought on in the mountainous areas of the country, harassed by German forces. Krisko was protected by the partisans until February 1945, when he contacted the advancing Red Army.

Post-war, he joined the newly-formed Czechoslovak Air Force, serving as CO of the 1st Air Regiment. However, prior to its re-equipment with modern Soviet MiG-15 jet fighters, Maj Krisko was removed from his post and dismissed from the air force for political reasons – he was a veteran of the fight *against* the Red Army in World War 2. Krisko subsequently found long-term employment with the forestry commission in Malacky and Bratislava. He died on 5 February 1988 in Bratislava, aged 72.

Bf 109E-7 (Wk-Nr 6474) 'White 12' of porucik Vladimir Krisko, 13(*slow*)./JG 52, Maikop, Kuban, November 1942

This aircraft was used to train Slovak fighter pilots at Karup-Grøve airfield, in occupied Denmark, and then returned with them to Slovakia. It subsequently became one the No 13 Sqn *Emils* transferred to the eastern front in October 1942, where it was usually flown by deputy CO Vladimir Krisko. It was written off on 10 January 1943 when it crashed on take-off from Krasnodar with catnik Jozef Vincur at the controls.

SPECIFICATION

Messerschmitt Bf 109E
(all dimensions and performance data for Bf 109E-3)

TYPE:	single-engined monoplane fighter
ACCOMMODATION:	pilot
DIMENSIONS:	length 28 ft 0 in (8.55 m)
	wingspan 32 ft 4.5 in (9.87 m)
	height 8 ft 2 in (2.49 m)
WEIGHTS:	empty 4189 lb (1900 kg)
	maximum take-off 5875 lb (2665 kg)
PERFORMANCE:	maximum speed 348 mph (560 kmh)
	range 410 miles (660 km)
	powerplant Daimler-Benz DB 601Aa
	output 1175 hp (876 kW)
ARMAMENT:	two Rheinmetall Borsig MG 17 7.9 mm machine guns in the upper cowling, two MG FF 20 mm cannon in wings; some aircraft had an additional MG FF 20 mm cannon in the propeller hub; fighter-bomber variant provision for carriage of one 551-lb (250 kg) bomb under fuselage
FIRST FLIGHT DATE:	June 1937 (Bf 109 V10)
OPERATORS:	Bulgaria, Croatia, Germany, Rumania, Slovakia, Spain, Switzerland, Yugoslavia
PRODUCTION:	approximately 4000

Designed to meet a 1934 *Reichluftfahrtministerium* (RLM) requirement for a single-seat monoplane fighter, the original Bf 109 V1 was the winning competitor in a 'fly off' that involved three other designs from proven German aviation companies. Light and small, the first production-standard Bf 109s (B-1 models) to enter service in early 1937 proved their worth during the Spanish Civil War. By the time Germany invaded Poland in September 1939, the re-engined Bf 109E was rolling off the Messerschmitt production line in great quantity, the now-familiar airframe being paired up with the powerful Daimler-Benz DB 601 engine. Built in huge numbers, and in a great array of sub-variants for the fighter, reconnaissance, fighter-bomber and shipboard fighter roles, the Bf 109E proved to be the master of all its European contemporaries bar the Spitfire Mk I/II, to which it was considered an equal. Aside from fighting over Poland, the E-model saw combat throughout the *Blitzkrieg* of 1940 and then the Battle of Britain which followed, in the Balkans in 1941 and in the opening phases of the North African and Soviet campaigns. A number of Germany's Axis partners were also supplied with second-hand Bf 109Es in 1941-42, including Slovakia, which flew more than 20 battle-weary *Emils* on the eastern front and in homeland defence well into 1943.

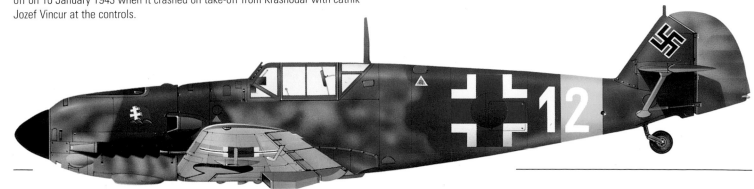

'Palm Sunday Massacre'

'I fired two bursts into two more Ju 52s, again in the leading formation. They both burst into flames.'

The single most successful mission ever flown by P-40 Warhawk pilots of the USAAF took place on 18 April 1943 in an action known popularly as the 'Palm Sunday Massacre'. This episode occurred in the closing days of the Tunisian campaign, by which point Axis forces had been squeezed tighter and tighter into the Cape Bon area, their cause clearly lost. For several weeks before Palm Sunday, large formations of Luftwaffe transport aircraft had been shuttling back and forth between Cape Bon and Sicily. Initially, the primary purpose of these flights was to carry reinforcements and war material to North Africa – later they began evacuating troops.

Considering the air superiority enjoyed by the Allies over Tunisia, it was just a matter of time before the shuttle flights began to run into trouble. In encounters on 10 and 11 April off Cape Bon, P-38s of the Twelfth Air Force had shot down 50 Ju 52/3m transports, and it was also reported that American B-25 medium bombers on a shipping sweep over the Mediterranean had downed a number of Junkers transports with their turret guns.

In the early hours of the morning on 18 April, intelligence reports reaching the 57th FG headquarters at El Djem indicated

Capt Roy E 'Deke' Whittaker of the 65th FS emerged from the 'Palm Sunday Massacre' as the top-scoring ace of the 57th FG. His four victories that day boosted his total to seven kills, which he displayed on his P-40F-1 41-14081 *Miss Fury* (*via Carl Molesworth*)

that the Germans were planning a big airlift of key personnel from Tunis to Sicily. Col Art Salisbury, CO of the 57th FG, duly began sending out patrols during the day, but time after time they returned to base with nothing to report.

At 1705 hrs yet another patrol was launched, some 48 P-40s of the 64th, 65th, 66th and 314th FSs heading out from El Djem. With RAF Spitfire Mk Vs of No 92 Sqn flying top cover, the formation encountered a huge V-formation of Ju 52/3m transports, with an escort of Bf 109Gs, flying low over the Bay of Tunis in a northeasterly direction. The P-40s attacked, and in the melee that followed Capt Roy E Whittaker of the 65th FS scored four of the USAAF's 76 confirmed victories, bringing his personal

One of the original pilots in the 65th PS/57th PG, 2Lt Roy E 'Deke' Whittaker is seen here with one of his squadron's P-40Es in early 1942. Whittaker would go on to score seven victories in North Africa (*via Carl Molesworth*)

tally to seven, and making him the highest-scoring ace in the legendary 'First in the Blue' 57th FG.

Whittaker, in Col Art Salisbury's P-40F 'White 01', was leading a flight of 65th FS fighters as part of the middle cover formation. He gave the following account of the battle;

'I attacked the Ju 52s from astern at high speed and fired at two aeroplanes in the leading formation. The bursts were short, and the only effect I saw was pieces flying off the cabin of the second ship. I pulled away, circled to the right and made my second attack. I fired two bursts into two more Ju 52s, again in the leading formation. They both burst into flames. The second flew a little distance and then crashed into the water. I lost sight of the first and didn't see it hit.

'I then made a third pass and sent a good burst into the left of the formation at another Junkers. As I pulled away, it crashed into the water. By that time the Me 109s were among us. As I pulled up to the left, I saw a '109 dive through an element of four Warhawks and I tagged on his underside and gave him a long burst in the belly. He crashed into the sea from 1000 ft.

'I then joined up with some Warhawks that were Lufberying with six Me 109s. I met one of these fighters with a quartering attack and hit him with a short burst. Pieces flew from the aeroplane and he started smoking, but climbed out of the fight. It was a fighter pilot's dream. I'd never seen such a complete massacre of the enemy in my life.'

Whittaker was not at the controls of his assigned machine on 18 April 1943. He instead got stuck into the Ju 52/3ms flying the 57th FG's most colourful P-40F, Col Art Salisbury's 'White 01'. As this photograph of the aircraft's nose clearly reveals, this machine (whose serial remains unknown) was decorated with all three unit badges – it is believed that this trio of markings also appeared on the starboard side of the Warhawk as well (*via Carl Molesworth*)

PILOT BIOGRAPHY – ROY WHITTAKER

Roy 'Deke' Whittaker is remembered as the leading ace of the 57th FG, one of the USAAF's most storied units of World War 2.

Born in Knoxville, Tennessee, on 6 July 1919, Roy Eugene Whittaker graduated from the University of Tennessee prior to joining the US Army Air Corps on 15 March 1941. His leadership abilities stood out from the beginning, as he was appointed Commandant of Cadets of Class 41-I, completing flight training at Kelly Field, Texas, on 12 December 1941 – less than a week after the United States entered World War 2. He briefly remained at Kelly Field as an instructor after receiving his wings, before transferring to the 65th PS of the recently-formed 57th PG, which was training for combat in the Curtiss P-40 Warhawk.

Lt Whittaker and the rest of the air echelon of the 57th left for North Africa aboard the aircraft carrier USS *Ranger* in June 1942. Arriving off the Gold Coast port of Accra in early July, the 57th FG promptly made history by becoming the first USAAF fighter group to launch at strength from an aircraft carrier. Whittaker's P-40F Warhawk was the second of 72 aeroplanes off *Ranger's* deck that day. After a brief period flying with the RAF to gain combat experience, Whittaker commenced full-scale operations with the 57th FG when the El Alamein offensive opened in late October 1942. The future ace destroyed an Italian C.202 for his first aerial victory on 26 October, and added a second Italian fighter to his score the following day. His first victory over a German aircraft – a Bf 109G – came on 11 January 1943.

Recently promoted to captain, Whittaker took part in the famous 'Palm Sunday Massacre' mission of 18 April 1943, shooting down three Ju 52/3m transports and a Bf 109 off Cape Bon, Tunisia. This brought his score to seven confirmed victories, which was the highest total amassed by any 57th FG pilot during the war. Whittaker completed his combat tour in June 1943, having flown 87 combat missions. He saw out the rest of the war as an instructor in the US.

Post-war, Whittaker became a career US Air Force officer, retiring in 1973 with the rank of colonel. He died on 24 June 1989.

P-40F-1 41-14081 'White 43' of Capt Roy E 'Deke' Whittaker, 65th FS/57th FG, Hani Main, Tunisia, April-May 1943

Whittaker, top ace of the 57th FG, flew two similarly-marked Warhawks during his combat tour, and this was the second of them. The first was transferred to the 66th FS in December 1942 and renumbered 'White 96'. This aeroplane carries Whittaker's full score of seven victories, and it also displays the 65th FS 'Fighting Cocks' badge on the nose. Note that swastikas have been used to mark all of Whittaker's kills, although two of his victims were Italian aircraft. His most successful combat mission was on 18 April 1943, when he shot down three Ju 52/3m transports and a Bf 109 during the 'Palm Sunday Massacre'. *Miss Fury* was lost in October 1943, several months after Whittaker had completed his combat tour.

SPECIFICATION

Curtiss P-40F/L Kittyhawk/Warhawk
(all dimensions and performance data for P-40F)

TYPE: single-engined monoplane fighter

ACCOMMODATION: pilot

DIMENSIONS: length 33 ft 4 in (10.16 m)
wingspan: 37 ft 4 in (11.38 m)
height 12 ft 4 in (3.76 m)

WEIGHTS: empty 7000 lb (3175 kg)
maximum take-off 8500 lb (3855 kg)

PERFORMANCE: maximum speed 364 mph (586 kmh)
range 1500 miles (2414 km) with external drop tank
powerplant Packard Merlin V-1650-1
output 1300 hp (1104 kW)

ARMAMENT: six Colt Browning 0.50-in machine guns in the wings; one 500-lb (227 kg) bomb under the fuselage or two 100-lb (45 kg) under the wings

FIRST FLIGHT DATE: 30 June 1941

OPERATORS: Australia, South Africa, UK, USA, USSR

PRODUCTION: 2000

The poor performance of the Allison-engined P-40 at altitudes in excess of 20,000 ft had been a cause of great concern to the Allies from the start of the war. In an attempt to solve this problem, Curtiss re-engined the second production P-40D airframe with a Rolls-Royce Merlin 28. Flown for the first time on 30 June 1941 (as the XP-40F), the fighter's performance was deemed to have been improved sufficiently enough for orders for 1311 P-40Fs to be placed. These were powered by Packard-built V-1650-1 Merlins, rated at 1300 hp for take-off. Boasting a similar six-gun armament to the Allison-engined P-40E/K, the F-model also subsequently adopted the lengthened fuselage of the P-40K-10. An order for 330 P-40Fs was placed with Curtiss for Commonwealth air forces, and some 117 of these were supplied to the RAF, RAAF and the SAAF, with 100 of the remaining airframes going to the USSR. The final Merlin-engined variant was the P-40L, which had two guns removed and its fuel capacity reduced in an effort to save overall weight – 700 L-models were built. Some 300 surviving P-40F/Ls were re-engined with Allison V-1710-81s and redesignated P-40Rs in 1944 because of a shortage of Merlin spares. P-40F/Ls saw action with the Allies in North Africa and the Mediterranean, the Far East, the Pacific and on the eastern front.

DEFENDERS OF LING LING

'There were 30 or so of them, all fighters, and it was impossible to catch anyone asleep or by himself, so it was mighty tough going for a while.'

At 1444 hrs on 24 April 1943, the Japanese 1st Air Brigade, located at bases in the Hankow area, launched 44 Ki-43 'Oscars' of the 25th and 33rd *Sentais* on a raid against the American base at Ling Ling, in China. The weather had been bad all month, with days of low cloud and heavy rain blighting the area, but on this Saturday before Easter the conditions improved just enough for the Japanese to mount their attack. They made the 200-mile run southwest to Ling Ling, with plans to pass east of the base and then turn back toward the northwest so as to carry out a surprise attack from an unlikely direction. By employing such a ruse, the 'Oscar' pilots hoped to catch as many American aircraft as possible on the ground, and then to strafe them at will.

Unfortunately for the Japanese, the Chinese air warning net had been tracking them from the moment they took off from Hankow, thus giving the 23rd FG's 75th FS plenty of time to launch 14 P-40Ks in defence of its base at Ling Ling. Leading one of the Warhawk flights was Capt Johnny Hampshire, flying his P-40K-1 42-45232 'White 161'.

The American pilots intercepted the attackers about ten miles southeast of Ling Ling and joined battle immediately. According to the 75th FS squadron history, the Japanese went into a formation that the Americans called the 'squirrel cage' (similar to a Lufbery

Capt Johnny Hampshire smiles for the camera at Ling Ling soon after claiming his sixth kill on 1 April 1943. He is sat in his P-40K-1 42-45232 'White 161' (*via Carl Molesworth*)

Taken at around the same time as the photograph on page 92, this shot again shows Johnny Hampshire with his P-40K-1 'White 161' at Ling Ling in early April 1943. He would add seven more victories, and tie with AVG ace Bob Neale as the top-scoring American P-40 pilot of the war, before being killed in action in this aeroplane on 2 May 1943. In 1998 the airport at Grants Pass, Oregon (Hampshire's hometown), was renamed in his honour (*via Carl Molesworth*)

circle). Whenever a P-40 pilot would attempt to take a shot at a Ki-43, there would be several more 'Oscars' ready to swing in behind him. The Japanese pilots showed unusually good discipline, making it difficult for the Warhawk pilots to stay in a firing position long enough to get off a telling burst. Nevertheless, Johnny Hampshire was able to confirm one 'Oscar' destroyed, and three other pilots in the 75th also got single kills. No P-40s were lost, although the Japanese claimed three destroyed.

The fight lasted an extraordinarily long 55 minutes, and toward the end of it a twin-engined 'fighter' (most likely a Ki-46 'Dinah' of the 18th Independent Air Squadron) flew over Ling Ling and dropped leaflets on the base.

The following account of this engagement was included in a letter that Johnny Hampshire wrote home just 24 hours after he had downed the 'Oscar' (which he had misidentified as a Zero) and the 'Dinah' for his seventh and eighth victories;

'Yesterday, the Japanese paid us another visit, and it was a dilly. They really sent in the first team this time, and they had the most beautiful air discipline I have ever seen. There were 30 (sic) or so of them, all fighters, and it was impossible to catch anyone asleep or by himself, so it was mighty tough going for a while. The fight was a fairly long one, and just when it was ending, one of their twin-engined fighters flew over and dropped out a bunch of pamphlets (the pamphlet challenged the American air forces to a "decisive air battle" – Author).

'The monkey that dropped the pamphlets ran into a little hard luck on the way home. For a while it looked like I'd never catch him, but I finally did after chasing him a hundred miles. So that ended the show for that day. I got two for the day.'

Groundcrewmen from the 75th FS take a break from refuelling aircraft on the flightline at Hengyang. The P-40K at left is fitted with mounting brackets for small bombs beneath its wing. Note also that the outline for the shark's tongue has been chalked on, although it has not yet been painted, and that neither P-40K has a shark's eye on its nose (*via Carl Molesworth*)

PILOT BIOGRAPHY – JOHN HAMPSHIRE

Daring and skilful, Johnny Hampshire earned a place in history by tying for the distinction of being the USAAF's top-scoring P-40 pilot of World War 2.

John Frederick Hampshire Jr was born in Grants Pass, Oregon, on 16 May 1919, the son of a highway construction contractor. He graduated from Grants Pass High School in 1936 and attended Oregon State College, soon developing a keen interest in flying. Accepted for pilot training in the US Army Air Corps shortly after the war broke out in Europe, Hampshire received instruction at Hamilton Field, California, and then graduated from Kelly Field, Texas, on 4 October 1940.

The newly minted second lieutenant was assigned to the Panama Canal Zone, where he honed his skills as a fighter pilot flying P-36s for 21 months with the 24th PS/16th PG. One of 20 fighter pilots transferred from Panama to China for frontline duty, Hampshire joined the 75th FS/23rd FG at Kweilin in October 1942. His flying ability and aggressive nature paid off almost immediately. Hampshire, newly promoted to captain, scored his first two victories on 25 October when the China Air Task Force attacked Hong Kong for the first time. Just over a month later, on 27 November 1942, Hampshire reached the coveted status of ace when he shot down three more Japanese fighters on a bomber escort mission to Canton.

The 75th FS passed an uneventful winter in Kunming, but aerial action resumed in April 1943 when the squadron moved up to Ling Ling, and Hampshire was smack in the middle of it. He scored one of the unit's five victories on 1 April, and knocked down two more Japanese aeroplanes 23 days later. Then, on 28 April, he had his biggest day, destroying two fighters and a bomber (as well as claiming three probables) in a scramble from Kunming.

The 24-year-old Oregonian flew his final mission on 2 May 1943. Scrambled from Ling Ling once more, he shot down two Ki-43 'Oscars' but was then badly wounded in the stomach. He landed his P-40K wheels-up in the Hsiang River, but died before medical help could reach him. At the time of his death, Johnny Hampshire was the USAAF's top-scoring ace, with 13 confirmed victories.

P-40K-1 42-45232/'White 161' of Capt John F Hampshire Jr, 75th FS/23rd FG, China, April 1943

Johnny Hampshire served with the 24th PG in the Canal Zone prior to being posted to China in October 1942. The aggressive Oregonian wasted no time in getting amongst the enemy, scoring his first two victories on 25 October and three more on 12 November to become the first pilot to reach ace status in the 75th FS. It is likely that Hampshire claimed all of his victories, bar the first two, in 'White 161', and he was killed in action in this aircraft north of Changsha on 2 May 1943. The fighter was painted Dark Earth and Dark Green over Neutral Grey, and featured the white fuselage band of the 75th FS, in addition to red, white and blue pinwheel designs on its wheel hubs. Hampshire was the leading ace in the CBI with 13 confirmed victories at the time of his death.

SPECIFICATION

Curtiss P-40K Warhawk

TYPE:	single-engined monoplane fighter
ACCOMMODATION:	pilot
DIMENSIONS:	length 33 ft 4 in (10.16 m) wingspan 37 ft 4 in (11.38 m) height 12 ft 4 in (3.76 m)
WEIGHTS:	empty 6400 lb (2903 kg) maximum take-off 9350 lb (4246 kg)
PERFORMANCE:	maximum speed 363 mph (580 kmh) range 1600 miles (2560 km) with external drop tank powerplant Allison V-1710-73 output 1325 hp (1002 kW)
ARMAMENT:	six Colt Browning 0.50-in machine guns in the wings; one 500-lb (227 kg) bomb under the fuselage or two 100-lb (45 kg) under the wings
FIRST FLIGHT DATE:	early 1942
OPERATORS:	Australia, South Africa, UK, Canada, USA, USSR, China
PRODUCTION:	1300

Military historians have not always been kind to the Curtiss P-40, the US Army Air Force's frontline fighter at the start of America's involvement in World War 2. The P-40 was caught on the ground at Pearl Harbor and was badly mauled by Japanese A6M Zero fighters over the Philippines and Java. In the year that followed, P-40 pilots barely managed to hold the line in northern Australia and New Guinea until new fighters with higher performance became available. Yet in one remote corner of the war the P-40 Warhawk compiled a combat record as good as the finest fighter types of its era. In so doing, it captured the imagination and adoration of the American public as few warplanes ever have. These P-40s were the ones flown in the China-Burma-India (CBI) Theatre. Operated first by Claire Lee Chennault's legendary American Volunteer Group (AVG), and later by American and Chinese pilots of the Tenth and Fourteenth Air Forces, the P-40 simply dominated the skies over Burma and China. They were able to establish air superiority over free China, northern Burma and the Assam Valley of India in 1942, and they never relinquished it. Initially flying the surviving AVG Tomahawks and a handful of new P-40Es, in 1943 the first brand new K-model Warhawks arrived in the CBI, and the 23rd and 51st FGs made great use of these well into 1944, when they were replaced by P-40Ns and P-51B/Cs.

Warhawk Ace in a Day

'I then went after a "Betty" bomber, and on my first pass his right engine started burning.'

1Lt Joseph J Lesicka was one of the many young fighter pilots who trained in Hawaii prior to joining combat units engaged in the Pacific campaign. Assigned to the 44th FS/18th FG on Guadalcanal in February 1943, Lesicka scored nine confirmed victories in P-40s (*via Carl Molesworth*)

Some of the fiercest aerial fighting of the Pacific War occurred during the Allies' advance on New Georgia, in the Solomon Islands chain, as Japanese aerial forces on Bougainville attempted to deny the vital airfield at Munda to the Allies. US and Australian forces had invaded Rendova Island and New Georgia on 30 June 1943, triggering a new round of aerial battles over the Solomon chain. From then until Munda was captured on 5 August, the 44th FS/18th FG scored no fewer than 50.5 victories, creating seven aces. Amongst the latter was 1Lt Joseph J Lesicka, who had the rare distinction of scoring five confirmed victories to become an 'ace in a day'.

On 15 July 1943, a force of 27 Japanese G4M 'Betty' bombers, with 40-50 Zero escorts, was reported approaching Munda from the west. Some 44 Allied fighters responded to the alert, including seven new lightweight P-40Ms from the 44th FS/18th FG which had taken off from Munda to fly a patrol over nearby Rendova Island.

Receiving the call that a large enemy formation had been spotted heading for their base, the Warhawk pilots hastily climbed to 15,000 ft over Kolombangara, where they encountered A6M Zero fighters that had been scattered by an earlier clash with Marine F4Us. Flight leader, and future eight-victory ace, Capt Frank Gaunt led his P-40s in a diving attack, taking a hasty shot at a Zero which apparently missed. The Japanese fighter then turned in front of

Gaunt's element leader, 1Lt Lesicka, who promptly shot it down from behind. Within the next few seconds all seven of the Warhawks became involved in a running dogfight that ranged eastward toward Vella LaVella and then back to Rendova. The P-40 pilots duly claimed a total of 12.5 victories for the loss of just one Warhawk.

This is Joseph Lesicka's terse personal account of his part in the swirling aerial battle;

'I got one Zero with a shot from the rear. I then saw a torpedo bomber and overran him on my first pass, but smoked him, and on my next pass I blew him up. I then went after a "Betty" bomber, and on my first pass his right engine started burning. An F4U made a pass, and he went down on my second pass, giving me the "Betty". I then took two Zeros off a P-40's tail – I got both of them, and one was shot with only one gun.'

1Lt Lesicka claimed 4.5 victories following the mission, but he was duly given credit for all five. With or without the additional half share for the 'Betty' (which the P-40 pilot claimed had been damaged by the F4U that he saw attacking it first), Lesicka 'made ace' on the mission, since he had scored three confirmed victories during the preceding month. By war's end he had increased his tally to nine destroyed and one damaged.

During the summer of 1943 the tail surfaces of Warhawks in the Solomon Islands were painted solid white to distinguish them from inline-engined Ki-61 'Tony' fighters of the Japanese Army Air Force. Shown here at 'Fighter Strip Two' on Guadalcanal, 'White 116' was the regular aircraft of 44th FS ace 1Lt Henry E Matson and 'White 111' was flown by ace 1Lt Jack Bade (*via Carl Molesworth*)

Joe Lesicka of the 44th FS scored five victories in a single mission on 15 July 1943 flying his P-40M 'White 125' *Gypsy Rose Lee*. The top-scoring Warhawk ace of the squadron with nine confirmed victories at the end of his first tour, Lesicka returned to the 44th FS as CO in 1944, and later moved to 18th FG headquarters (*via Carl Molesworth*)

PILOT BIOGRAPHY – JOSEPH LESICKA

'Jumping Joe' Lesicka earned the rare title of 'ace in a day' by receiving credit for five Japanese aircraft destroyed in a single mission on 15 July 1943. The fact that he accomplished this achievement while flying a P-40 Warhawk makes it all the more noteworthy.

A native of Los Angeles, California, Joseph J Lesicka was born on 19 December 1919. One of the thousands of young Americans who signed up for military duty in the weeks following the surprise Japanese attack on Pearl Harbor, he joined the US Army Air Corps in January 1942 for flight training. Lesicka received his wings at Luke Field, Arizona, as part of Class 42-G on 25 July 1942 and was sent to fly P-39s in Hawaii with the 45th FS/15th FG. In April 1943 he was posted to Guadalcanal's 'Fighter Strip Two' as a replacement pilot for the 44th FS/18th FG, which was equipped with P-40F Warhawks.

Lesicka's first opportunity to score came on 16 June 1943, when a large formation of Japanese 'Val' dive-bombers, with a swarm of Zero escorts, attempted to attack Allied shipping off Guadalcanal. More than 100 US fighters rose to the challenge, among them Lesicka and the 44th FS. The battle raged for an hour, netting the American pilots more than 40 victories. Lesicka's share was one 'Val' destroyed – closing in a dive from about 600 yards, he gave the aircraft several bursts of fire that sent it flaming into the sea.

Exactly two weeks later, while covering the Allied landings at Rendova Island, 1Lt Lesicka shot down an unidentified enemy 'float biplane', and he followed that on 12 July with a Zero destroyed over Munda. Then, on 15 July, came the next big aerial battle for the 44th FS in which Lesicka was credited with three Zeros, a 'Betty' and a 'Kate' torpedo bomber destroyed to join the long list of 44th FS aces. He scored his final victory (a Zero destroyed near Rendova) on 7 August 1943, and continued to serve in the 44th FS until completing his combat tour on 6 February 1944. Promoted to captain, Lesicka returned to the squadron (now flying P-38Ls) as its commanding officer in January 1945, and then transferred to the 18th FG headquarters the following month. He claimed an 'Oscar' damaged over Mandai airfield, in the Celebes, on 22 June 1945 while flying a P-38L borrowed from the 44th FG, and this proved to be his final aerial engagement of the war.

With the end of the conflict, Capt Lesicka left the service in 1946. He died in 1990.

P-40M (serial unknown) 'White 125' of Capt Joseph J Lesicka, 44th FS/18th FG, Munda, August 1943

Lesicka had already scored three victories in four months with the 44th FS when he took off on a mission over the invasion beach at Munda, on New Georgia Island. His patrol met a large formation of Japanese bombers and fighters, and in a hectic 20-minute engagement he shot down five enemy aircraft. Lesicka was the second 44th FS pilot to become an 'ace in a day', as 1Lt Elmer Wheadon had accomplished this rare feat on 1 July 1943. Lesicka's aircraft was named after burlesque star Gypsy Rose Lee, this being a reference to the fact that the M-model Warhawk was 'stripped' of weight in an attempt to improve performance. It also had a diving eagle design painted on its white wheel hubs.

SPECIFICATION

Curtiss P-40M Warhawk

TYPE:	single-engined monoplane fighter
ACCOMMODATION:	pilot
DIMENSIONS:	length 33 ft 4 in (10.16 m) wingspan 37 ft 4 in (11.38 m) height 12 ft 4 in (3.76 m)
WEIGHTS:	empty 6470 lb (2910 kg) maximum take-off 9100 lb (4210 kg)
PERFORMANCE:	maximum speed 360 mph (576 kmh) range 1600 miles (2560 km) with external drop tank powerplant Allison V-1710-81 output 1200 hp (895 kW)
ARMAMENT:	six Colt Browning 0.50-in machine guns in the wings; one 500-lb (227 kg) bomb under the fuselage or two 100-lb (45 kg) under the wings
FIRST FLIGHT DATE:	late 1942
OPERATORS:	Australia, South Africa, New Zealand, UK, USA, USSR
PRODUCTION:	600

As the United States Army's first-line fighter aircraft in overseas service in 1941, the P-40 bore the brunt of the early Japanese attacks in the Pacific, beginning with the devastating raid on Pearl Harbor. Its lack of success against the Japanese in the opening weeks of the war saddled the P-40 with a reputation as an underachieving dog of an aircraft, and to many Americans it became a symbol of their nation's lack of preparedness for war. It is true that the P-40 squadrons were rendered ineffective by the surprise attack on Pearl Harbor, and were completely wiped out in the Philippines and Java. This came at a time when the Allied nations were grasping for any tiny shred of good news from the war fronts, and this made the P-40's failures in the Pacific all the more difficult to bear. The aircraft's reputation suffered while the American armed forces struggled to figure out how to fight the modern air war that had been thrust upon them. Fortunately the P-40 pilots of 1942-43 turned out to be quick learners, for although the aircraft was lacking in two key elements of fighter performance – rate of climb and service ceiling – it boasted a robust airframe, heavy armament, a good turn of speed in level flight and the ability to out-dive any aircraft in Japanese service. Warhawks remained in the fight as the tide turned against the Japanese in the Pacific, and by war's end, USAAF P-40 pilots in-theatre had been credited with 610.5 confirmed victories over Japanese aircraft

ARR ACE

'I see the target growing in my gunsight. Now! Simultaneously, I press the cannon button with my thumb and the machine gun trigger with my index finger.'

On 6 June 1944, Locotenent aviator Ion Dobran of the élite *Escadrila* 48 *vânătoare, Grupul* 9 *vânătoare,* flying his Bf 109G-6 'Yellow 22', surprised two USAAF P-51Cs of the 317th FS/325th FG heading for the USSR at high altitude. In the ensuing battle, he successfully attacked Mustang 42-103519, flown by six-kill ace 2Lt Barrie Davis, but was forced by the other (42-103501, flown by 11-kill ace 1Lt Wayne Lowry) to land after a long chase from 20,000 ft down to ground level. The Rumanian pilot survived the crash landing, but his *Gustav* needed extensive repairs.

Due to a lack of witnesses, Dobran's ninth aerial victory remained a probable – 2Lt Davis struggled on to Mirgorod, in the Ukraine, where he successfully landed his Mustang, minus its canopy and with its tail half shot off. Dobran finished the war with 15 victories, ranking him 23rd in the unofficial list of ARR (Royal Rumanian Air Force) aces. The following edited description of the action is taken from his wartime diary;

Lt av Ion Dobran – dubbed 'The Fakir' by his fellow pilots – poses with his late-production Bf 109G-6 on a soaked Slovak airfield in the spring of 1945. One of the last surviving Rumanian Bf 109 aces from this era, Gen av (ret) Dobran recently published a personal diary containing vivid details of his wartime experiences, which included 74 aerial battles and 15 ARR victories (*via Dénes Bernád*)

Sat in the snug confines of the cockpit of his beloved Bf 109G-6 in the summer of 1944, Lt av Ion Dobran prepares to do battle with the massed ranks of the USAAF's Fifteenth Air Force in the skies over Rumania (*via Dénes Bernád*)

'We scramble for our first encounter with the Americans, and in the haste prior to us taking off, I signal to (Adj maj av Ioan) Panaite to join me as my wingman. He tries to keep up with me, but soon falls behind and joins another patrol. We climb over Tecuci airfield, waiting for instructions from "Albatross" radio station HQ. The latter soon tells us that enemy aeroplanes are heading towards "Independenta" (Galati).

'I just manage to spot the Americans flying away from us at a greater height – they look like sparkles in the sky. I approach them slowly by gaining altitude, although I arrive over Galati too late. I can see that the airfield and railway tunnel have been seriously bombed. I then spot two red-nosed aeroplanes flying at my left, slightly below me. Could they be Bf 109Gs of *Escadrila* 56? I fly parallel with them. Suddenly, I recognise their silhouettes. They are American Mustangs. Finally, the moment I have been waiting for!

'I carefully scout the area behind me. I am alone. I gain altitude and then gently dive towards them with increased speed. Now there is a four-ship patrol in front of me. I know that one against four means almost certain suicide. Nevertheless, I attack. I see the target growing in my gunsight. Now! Simultaneously, I press the cannon button with my thumb and the machine gun trigger with my index finger. Fire streams erupt from my cowling and spinner. I correct the aim slightly with the help of tracer bullets. At first, the American does not seem to react. Then, hit, he slides underneath the other aircraft.

'Instinctively looking behind, I spot the other Mustangs approaching. I take the classical escape method – a dive, then recovery. The three Mustangs are stuck to my tail. Only one is

dangerously close, however. Apparently he has greater speed and climbs better. He keeps sticking to my tail, no matter what I do. I try another sudden climb, then, like a giant hammer, the first hits. Others follow, without exploding. I spot a thin white stream on the left side of the fuselage. Instinctively, I reduce engine revolutions, intending to bail out, but decide to put my crippled machine down anywhere, just to escape my deadly foes. I lower my undercarriage and land on unknown terrain. The ground is soft, slowing me abruptly. Fearing the American might strafe, I jump out and look up. I cannot see anything. Only the dying roar of an engine can be faintly heard departing eastwards.'

A group photo of *Grupul* 9 *vânătoare* pilots, taken after VE-Day at Miskolc airfield, in Hungary, on 31 July 1945. They are, standing from left to right, Lt av Stefan Octavian Ciutac (11 victories), Lt av Ion Dobran (15), Adj av Constantin Ursache (11), *Grup* CO Cpt av Emil Georgescu, (eight), Lt av Constantin Rosariu (33), Cpt av Ioan Micu (13), Lt av Mihai Lucaci (no score) and Lt av Mircea Senchea (nine). The two pilots in front of the group are Lt av Ion Galea (12+) and Adj rez av Ion Mălăcescu (21+). Note the long row of war-weary Bf 109Gs neatly lined up in the background (*via Dénes Bernád*)

PILOT BIOGRAPHY – ION DOBRAN

Ion Dobran was born on 5 February 1919 in the Rumanian town of Văleni-Podgoria. Following graduation from the elementary school in Bucharest, he enrolled into the Military High School, located in Târgu Mures. Later joining the Flying School for Officers in Cotroceni-Bucharest, Sublocotenent aviator (Second Lieutenant airman) Ion Dobran received his wings on 10 May 1941. Once an accomplished fighter pilot, Slt av Dobran was assigned to IAR 80-equipped *Grupul* 9 *vânătoare* (9th Fighter Group) of *Flotila* 1 *vânătoare* (1st Fighter Flotilla) – the mainstay fighter unit of the *Aeronautica Regală Română*.

In the spring of 1943, an influx of modern German equipment allowed *Grupul* 9 *vânătoare* to swap its obsolescent IAR 80s for superior Bf 109Gs. By August the Rumanians had mastered their new mounts sufficiently enough for the unit to be sent to the eastern front. Following several fruitless encounters with the numerically superior enemy, Slt av Dobran claimed his first victory (although it was never confirmed) on 6 September over an Il-2 which had just attacked his airfield at Bliznets. He scored his first fully credited victory only two days later, also over a *Shturmovik*, in the same location. His last kill of the year was achieved over a Yak fighter near Bolshoy Tokmak on 25 September.

In early 1944, *Grupul* 9 *vânătoare* retreated to Lepetika, and on 26 February Dobran destroyed one of six Yaks he encountered northeast of Krivoy Rog. His unit returned to Tecuci airfield, in Rumania, just days later. Subsequently promoted to Locotenent (First Lieutenant), Dobran downed a La-5 on 11 April and shared in the destruction of an A-20 Boston four days later. He had claimed three more unconfirmed kills by the end of May. In June Lt av Dobran was made CO of *Escadrila* 48 *vânătoare*. That same month he clashed with American fighters for the first time, downing a P-51 Mustang on the 6th and a P-38 Lightning on the 26th.

On 20 August 1944, the Red Army launched a huge offensive on the Rumanian front, and Dobran found himself in the thick of the battle right from the start, downing a Yak fighter while providing air cover for Henschel Hs 129s. Three days later Rumania switched sides, and following the royal coup, Dobran participated in the defence of the capital against Luftwaffe bombers. On 25 August, he downed a He 111 bomber of KG 4 over Bucharest, which was to be his ninth, and last, confirmed aerial kill. From 7 September Dobran and his 9th Fighter Group participated in the anti-Axis campaign in Transylvania and then in Hungary proper, ending the war in Slovakia in May 1945.

By then Ion Dobran had flown 340 combat sorties, participated in 74 aerial combats and been shot down three times. Staying in the air force until 1952, he finally retired in 1973 following a 21-year-career flying for Rumania's national airline, TAROM. Dobran, one of the last survivors of the ace *vânători*, currently lives in Bucharest.

SPECIFICATION

Messerschmitt Bf 109G
(all dimensions and performance data for Bf 109G-6)

TYPE:	single-engined monoplane fighter
ACCOMMODATION:	pilot
DIMENSIONS:	length 29 ft 7.5 in (9.03 m)
	wingspan 32 ft 6.5 in (9.92 m)
	height 8 ft 2.5 in (2.50 m)
WEIGHTS:	empty 5893 lb (2673 kg)
	maximum take-off 7496 lb (3400 kg)
PERFORMANCE:	maximum speed 386 mph (621 kmh)
	range 620 miles (998 km) with external tank
	powerplant Daimler-Benz DB 605AM
	output 1800 hp (1342 kW)
ARMAMENT:	one Rheinmetall Borsig MK 108 20 mm cannon in propeller hub and two Rheinmetall Borsig MG 131 13 mm machine guns in upper cowling, two Mauser MG 151 20 mm cannon in underwing gondolas (optional); provision for various underfuselage stores
FIRST FLIGHT DATE:	late summer 1941
OPERATORS:	Bulgaria, Croatia, Finland, Germany, Hungary, Italy, Rumania, Slovakia, Switzerland, Spain
PRODUCTION:	approximately 24,000 G-models and 1750 K-models

Apart from Slovakia, Rumania was the only other Axis power to attack the USSR alongside Germany on 22 June 1941. In August 1943, a new and more powerful enemy made its first appearance in Rumanian skies – the USAAF. From 1944, the *Aeronautica Regală Română* would be embroiled in a deadly fight with US aircraft as it struggled to defend its homeland. Rumania switched sides on 23 August 1944, leaving the surviving *vânători* to face the deadliest enemy of them all – the Luftwaffe. Throughout the conflict the primary fighter of the ARR was the Bf 109. The Rumanians initially operated both new and refurbished *Emils* from 1940, these being supplanted by war-weary examples given to them by the Luftwaffe following the invasion of the USSR in June 1941. By spring 1943, it was clear that Rumanian units were equipped with obsolete aircraft, and the appearance of a new generation of Soviet fighters obliged the Germans to equip the ARR with more modern aircraft. The first combat squadron to receive the Bf 109G was *Escadrila* 43 *vânătoare*, which was lent 44 brand new G-2/4s for frontline use only. Further G-6s were supplied following the sustained targeting of Rumanian industrial sites by the USAAF in early 1944, some 30 to 40 serviceable *Gustavs* providing the ARR with its most potent fighting force. Indeed, these machines continued to see action against the Germans and Hungarians following Rumania's unilateral switching of sides on 23 August 1944.

Bf 109G-6 'White 2' (possibly Wk-Nr. 166161) of *Escadrila* 47 *vânătoare*, *Grupul* 9 *vânătoare*, July 1944

Flown occasionally by Lt av Ion Dobran during the bloody summer of 1944, this aircraft was reputedly lost with his squadron CO, Căpitan aviator Gheorghe Popescu-Ciocănel, at the controls. The latter was shot down over Tecuci by Fifteenth Air Force P-51s on 26 July 1944. Badly-burned, Popescu-Ciocănel died ten days later in hospital, by which time he had been credited with 13 confirmed and one unconfirmed aircraft downed in 40+ aerial combats. Note the *Grupul* 9 *vânătoare Deßloch–Serbănescu* emblem on the engine cowling.

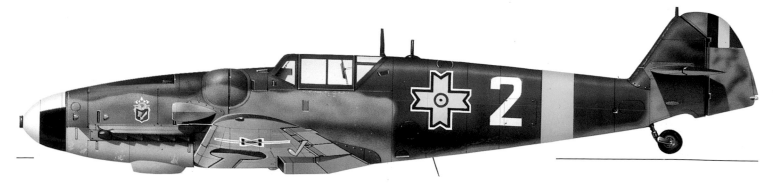

'PUMA' POTTYONDY

'The pilot tried to evade my shots with sudden jerking moves, but during my second attack a short 20 mm cannon burst gave him the coup de grâce.'

On the morning of 9 October 1944, two fighters of 102/2 'Ricsi' Fighter Squadron took off from their base at Munkács, in Hungary, and headed for Soviet supply routes supporting the tank battle in the Debrecen area. Control of this particular sector of the frontline had been entrusted by the Luftwaffe to this unit, which was opposed by a numerically superior Soviet force. The patrolling Messerschmitt fighters were flown by Capt László Pottyondy (in Bf 109G-6 'Red 5') and 1/Lt Ferenc Málnássy,

At this late stage of the war, Hungarian fighter pilots were finding it ever more difficult to get airborne in defence of their country, as Pottyondy explained;

'We had only two or three Bf 109Gs available to us. The Germans weren't much better off either, but we were more eager than them to prove that we were first-class pilots capable of achieving aerial victories if we had the weapons to fight with. We implored our Luftwaffe liaison officer for more aeroplanes, but all he did was shake his head in negation. We would have even accepted battle-worn "hand-me-down" aeroplanes if it meant we could fly, and that was exactly what the Germans eventually supplied us with.

Leading German ace (with 352 kills) Hauptmann Erich Hartmann (left), *Staffelkapitän* of 4./JG 52, poses with 13-kill ace Capt László Pottyondy in front of an aircraft from 102 FG. Sharing the airfield at Budaörs in November 1944, II./JG 52 and 102 FG regularly flew joint missions against the advancing Soviet forces. Indeed, on 17 November Erich Hartmann was flying as Pottyondy's wingman when each of them downed Bostons that were attacking targets around Budapest (*via György Punka*)

'One morning, the German liaison officer approached us with a broad smile on his face. He hinted that with pálinka (strong Hungarian fruit brandy, usually made from plums), many things could be solved! We got the message right away, and arranged for some pálinka to be brought in with the next Ju 52/3m transport. Once the coveted drink was in our possession, we flew to Kraków, in Poland, to receive the promised machines from the local repair workshop.

'The next day (9 October 1944) we returned home with four refurbished Bf 109Gs, fitted with new engines. Once back at base, we quickly started to paint Hungarian national markings on our mounts. However, we still hadn't finished the job when we received the order to scramble, as some 10 to 12 *Shturmoviks* had been spotted approaching the frontline. They were flying in a westerly direction at a height of about 2000 m, with a squadron of 12 La-5s some 1000 metres above them providing the fighter escort. The Lavochkins were tough adversaries, as their pilots were good and the aeroplane's radial engine could take plenty of punishment.

'I took off in "Red 5", with 1/Lt Málnássy as my wingman – we climbed in a westerly direction in view of the anticipated air battle. Once at combat altitude, we headed for the area indicated by the command post that had detected the Soviet aircraft and started looking for the enemy. It was not easy to navigate over the Carpathian Mountains, with compact forest covering the ground, and only a few guiding points available. Suddenly, we spotted the enemy formation flying in the opposite direction some 500 metres below us. They must have seen us, too, as the *Shturmoviks* started to

Its Hungarian markings applied in full colour, Bf 109G 'Red 2' was the regular mount of ace Lt László Pottyondy on the Soviet front during the autumn of 1944 (*via György Punka*)

descend, while the Lavochkins split into two formations and steered left and right, respectively. We then turned back westwards and caught up with the left Lavochkin formation.

'I cannot forget the dirty grey colour of the rearmost fighter. As I approached it from the rear, the La-5 grew large in my Revi gunsight. The pilot tried to evade my shots with sudden jerking moves, but during my second attack a short 20 mm cannon burst gave him the *coup de grâce*. After only five or six rounds, there was a sudden flash on the side of the La-5 and it started to smoke heavily. It banked to the left, then turned on its back and entered a steep dive. My eyes followed its descent until the fighter exploded on a hillside. After landing, I patted the side of my newly-acquired fighter. We had made a good deal with the pálinka.'

A 102 FG machine sits at Budaörs airfield during November 1944, its pilot sat astride the cockpit ready to take off at short notice. Note the engine crank handle sticking out of the side of the forward fuselage. The unit was heavily involved in flying missions against Soviet aircraft targeting Budapest when this shot was taken (*via György Punka*)

PILOT BIOGRAPHY – LÁSZLÓ POTTYONDY

Born in 1915, László Pottyondy graduated from the theology high school of Debrecen in 1934. Choosing a military career, he enrolled in the Ludovika Military Academy. Pottyondy graduated on 20 August 1938 and asked to be transferred to the fledgling *Magyar Királyi Honvéd Légierö* (MKHL, or Royal Hungarian Home Defence Air Force). After earning his wings, he was assigned to 1/2. 'Ludas Matyi' *vadászszázad* (1/2 Fighter Squadron), equipped with CR.32 biplanes.

In early 1941 Pottyondy was transferred to 2/3. 'Ricsi' *vadászszázad* (2/3 Fighter Squadron), which flew CR.42 biplanes. Based on Szamosfalva-Kolozsvár airfield, in northern Transylvania (today Someseni-Cluj, in Rumania), 1/Lt Pottyondy was made CO of the squadron's 2nd Flight. In April 1941 the squadron participated in the Hungarian invasion of Yugoslavia, operating alongside German forces campaign. Two months later the unit was in action again when the USSR was invaded, and on 27 June Pottyondy flew his first mission on the eastern front. Fulfilling bomber escort duties, the unit saw its first real action on 12 July, when its pilots reported seven aerial victories for no losses. Following this mêlée, Pottyondy was credited with an I-16 shot down over Dunayevtsi. Returning home later that month, Pottyondy's unit transitioned onto the Reggiane Re.2000 monoplane fighter.

Sent back to the eastern front in early 1942 with their obsolete Re.2000s, Pottyondy and his squadronmates soldiered on with the Reggianes during subsequent combat tours in 1943 and early 1944, when they at last received Bf 109Gs. Seeing more action against Soviet forces in the east in the summer of 1944, Pottyondy led the renamed and restructured 102/2 'Ricsi' Fighter Squadron into combat from Krehovtze airfield, near Stanislav, on 2 June. 1/Lt Pottyondy scored his first aerial victory as CO of the restructured unit on 15 September 1944, and he was successful again on 9 October. Two kills exactly three weeks later gave him ace status, and he added another victory to his growing tally on 1 November. His next kill came on the 17th of that same month, when he sortied with none other than Hauptmann Erich Hartmann, the greatest ace of them all, as his wingman.

Now fighting over Hungarian soil, Pottyondy and his men continued to engage Soviet aircraft as the pushed inexorably westward. More kills fell to the veteran ace in the new year, and on 8 March 1945 he claimed an Il-2 for his 13th, and last, kill of the war. By the time of the Axis surrender in May, Pottyondy had completed 119 combat sorties.

Initially taken prisoner by US forces, László Pottyondy eventually emigrated to America with his wife Eva. Moving to Little Rock, Arkansas, he befriended the owner (also of Hungarian descent) of the local airport, who helped him to get his pilot's licence. Pottyondy then found employment as a crop-dusting pilot, and he was killed in a flying accident in Little Rock in 1951.

SPECIFICATION

Messerschmitt Bf 109G
(all dimensions and performance data for Bf 109G-6)

TYPE:	single-engined monoplane fighter
ACCOMMODATION:	pilot
DIMENSIONS:	length 29 ft 7.5 in (9.03 m) wingspan 32 ft 6.5 in (9.92 m) height 8 ft 2.5 in (2.50 m)
WEIGHTS:	empty 5893 lb (2673 kg) maximum take-off 7496 lb (3400 kg)
PERFORMANCE:	maximum speed 386 mph (621 kmh) range 620 miles (998 km) with external tank powerplant Daimler-Benz DB 605AM output 1800 hp (1342 kW)
ARMAMENT:	one Rheinmetall Borsig MK 108 20 mm cannon in propeller hub and two Rheinmetall Borsig MG 131 13 mm machine guns in upper cowling, two Mauser MG 151 20 mm cannon in underwing gondolas; provision for various underfuselage and underwing stores
FIRST FLIGHT DATE:	late summer 1941
OPERATORS:	Bulgaria, Croatia, Finland, Germany, Hungary, Italy, Rumania, Slovakia, Switzerland, Spain
PRODUCTION:	approximately 24,000 G-models

In June 1941, Hungarian armed forces joined the Germans in the invasion of the Soviet Union, and pilots from 1/1 Fighter Squadron (FS) saw continuous action into 1942. Initially flying CR.42s and Re.2000s, the unit enjoyed only modest success until issued with used Bf 109F-4/Bs from late 1942 onwards. These aircraft were employed as fighter-bombers, 1/1 FS flying as part of I./JG 52 in an attempt to shore up the Italian front, which had been broken by the Soviets. In action during the Axis spring and summer offensives of 1943 in the Kharkov area, the Hungarian Bf 109Fs were supplanted by early-build *Gustavs*. By the time 5/1 FS fled east from Kiev in late September 1943, only a handful of F-models remained in service. The Hungarian Railway Carriage and Engineering Works had by then begun building Bf 109G-4/6s under licence, delivering some 92 aircraft by year-end. These machines were almost exclusively issued to home defence units, and production continued apace at the Györ plant until it was badly bombed by USAAF B-17s of the Fifteenth Air Force on 13 April 1944. With losses now made good from German stocks, Hungarian fighter units remained loyal to the Axis cause through to VE-Day. Indeed, 101 'Puma' Fighter Group pilots were flying late-build Bf 109G-10s from bases in Austria at war's end.

Bf 109G-6 'Blue 14' of Capt László Pottyondy, Commanding Officer of 102/2 'Ricsi' FS, Budaörs, Hungary, November 1944

Two Hungarian fighter squadrons were in action on the eastern front during the autumn of 1944, with 13-kill ace László Pottyondy commanding 102/2 FS. Despite being constantly outnumbered, and struggling with a chronic shortage of aircraft, veteran pilots from the unit claimed half a dozen kills in the final months of 1944. This particular machine boasts the unit's rarely-seen dog emblem on its cowling. Promoted to captain in late October, Pottyondy regularly led his squadron on combined missions with III./JG 52, which shared the unit's new base at Budaörs. Lacking aircraft, 102/2 FS was finally integrated into 101 FG as its eighth squadron in December 1944.

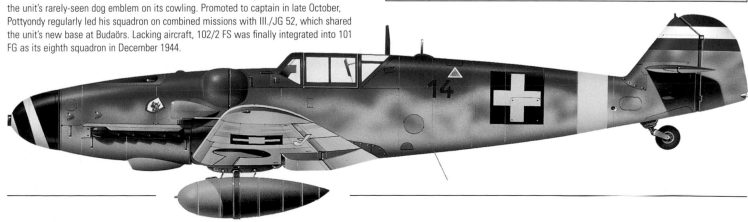

'ON MY OWN TIME'

'He was right in front of me at point-blank range. Two short bursts produced no apparent effect, but on the third burst the Jap disintegrated with a violent blast. Flying debris thundered against my P-38.'

'On 2 November 1944, I was leading a squadron flight of 14 P-38s out of Tacloban airstrip on a dive-bombing strike against Japanese shipping in Ormoc Bay, on the west side of Leyte. Intelligence reported a concentration of troop transports, with destroyer and cruiser escorts, landing troops in the area.

'Our strategy was to take the first six aircraft across the bay at low level, drawing naval ack-ack. This would permit the remaining aircraft, carrying 500-lb bombs, to make their attacks with minimum opposition. Although reports of enemy aircraft in sizeable numbers came in, we went unmolested during the first portion of the attack, and one of our pilots got a direct hit with a 500-lb bomb on a troopship.

'About the time decoy flights were pulling up at the far end of the bay, and the dive-bombing runs were almost over, enemy aircraft were spotted in several directions by our pilots. One was sighted at "six o'clock" to me. I went into a tight climbing turn to meet the enemy head-on. Since my wingman stayed glued to me during the turn, the enemy pilot lost his enthusiasm and broke off into a climbing turn. My position was better now, and the chase continued.

'Gradually, I gained on the Jap, climbing in the process to 16,000 ft. He was identifiable now as one of the new "Jack" fighters. He elected to enter a shallow dive, which against the P-38 was decidedly unwise. I needed full power for quite a while

Joint top-scoring P-40 pilot in V Fighter Command, Bob DeHaven continued his run of success in combat when his unit transitioned onto the P-38L in the late summer of 1944 (*via William Hess*)

Capt DeHaven poses with his elaborately marked P-38L (serial unknown) at Lingayen in June 1945. All of his aircraft were numbered '13', this particular machine being DeHaven's mount during his brief second tour in the SWPA in mid 1945. Note the dive-bombing guides in the form of black stripes marked on the wing leading edge inboard of the port engine (*via John Stanaway*)

to catch him, but at 10,000 ft, and indicating 400 mph, he was right in front of me at point-blank range. Two short bursts produced no apparent effect, but on the third burst the Jap disintegrated with a violent blast. Flying debris thundered against my P-38. My wind-shield was smothered in Japanese engine oil. I had to use my side vision and the careful direction of my wingman to get back to base.

'During the disassembly of my P-38, a large portion of one of the pilot's maps was found in one of the oil cooler scoops. This momento is today a prized possession. Another momento of this combat is a copy of orders sending me Stateside from the Philippines after 22 months overseas. They are dated 1 November 1944. My most memorable mission had been unknowingly on my own time.'

This account, written by 14-kill ace Bob DeHaven in the 1990s, details the demise of his penultimate victory on 2 November 1944. Assigned to the 49th Fighter Group's 7th Fighter Squadron, DeHaven was, on this occasion, flying an unidentified P-38L Lightning that had almost certainly been transferred into the group from either the 8th or 475th FGs as an attrition replacement during the fiercely fought Philippines campaign. The aircraft is seen in this artwork just seconds after flying through the fireball created by the exploding Mitsubishi J2M3 'Jack' fighter.

Lt Col Jerry Johnson (centre, back row) poses with fellow 49th FG HQ pilots at Lingayen soon after he had scored his final kill on 1 April 1945. Flanking the group CO in the back row are Majs George 'Choo-Choo' Laven (four kills) and Clay Tice, while in the front row, from left to right, are Capt Bob DeHaven (14 kills), Maj 'Wally' Jordan (six kills) and Capt James 'Duckbutt' Watkins (12 kills). Forming the backdrop to this group shot is Jerry Johnson's final Lightning – an unidentified P-38L-5 which was appropriately named *Jerry*. The fighter boasts his full tally of 25 kills, which included an RAAF Wirraway (shot down in error) and two Aleutian 'Rufes' that Johnson always claimed, but which were not officially recognised by the USAAF (*via John Stanaway*)

PILOT BIOGRAPHY – BOB DeHAVEN

Robert Marshall DeHaven was born on 13 January 1922 in San Diego, California. He enrolled in the Washington and Lee University in the late 1930s, but left prior to graduation in order to join the Army Reserves in February 1942. Earning his wings with Class 43-A at Luke Field, Arizona, on 4 January 1943, DeHaven transitioned onto the P-40 in Florida and was then sent to the Hawaii-based 73rd FS/318th FG. Units in action in the SWPA were desperately short of qualified pilots at this time, and DeHaven was duly transferred to V Fighter Command's 7th FS/49th FG in May 1943. Travelling firstly to Australia and then to New Guinea, the future ace eventually arrived at the unit's Dobodura base several weeks later.

DeHaven claimed his first kill on 14 July when he downed a 'Val' dive-bomber over Salamaua. Further successes followed in October, when he destroyed an 'Oscar' on the 17th and a 'Zeke' and a 'Tony' ten days later. DeHaven 'made ace' on 10 December with the destruction of a 'Tony', and within 48 hours another Ki-43 had fallen to his guns. The New Year started well for DeHaven, with a Ki-61 destroyed on 2 January and an 'Oscar' on the 23rd of the month. Another Ki-43 was downed on 15 March. He claimed a D4Y 'Judy' dive-bomber as his tenth, and last, P-40 victory on 7 May. DeHaven's success with the Warhawk made him equal top scorer (with Capt Ernest A Harris of the 8th FS/49th FG) on the type in V Fighter Command.

There was little opportunity for DeHaven to add to his tally during the summer of 1944, his squadron transitioning to the P-38 during this period. DeHaven's first Lightning score came on 29 October when he destroyed an 'Oscar' over Biliran Island, and his final trio of victories swiftly followed on 1, 2 and 4 November, when he claimed two 'Zekes' and a J2M 'Jack' fighter whilst patrolling over Leyte. Boosting his final tally to 14 kills, DeHaven was then sent home on leave. He returned to the 49th FG as group operations officer in 1945, but failed to add to his score prior to VJ-Day. By war's end DeHaven, who was the 7th FS's ranking ace, had flown 272 combat missions.

DeHaven joined the California Air National Guard post-war, acting as its P-80 acceptance test pilot. He transferred to the Air Force Reserve in 1950, from which he retired with the rank of colonel in 1965. In civilian life, DeHaven found employment with Hughes Aircraft Company in 1948, where he worked as an engineering test pilot and personal pilot to Howard Hughes. He eventually became an executive of the company, managing the flight test division for over 30 years. During that time DeHaven was elected a Fellow in the Society of Experimental Test Pilots, and also served as President of the American Fighter Aces Association.

SPECIFICATION

Lockheed P-38J/L Lightning

TYPE: twin-engined monoplane fighter

ACCOMMODATION: pilot

DIMENSIONS: length 37 ft 10 in (11.53 m)
wingspan 52 ft 0 in (15.85 m)
height 9 ft 10 in (3.00 m)

WEIGHTS: empty 12,800 lb (5791 kg)
maximum take-off 21,600 lb (9798 kg)

PERFORMANCE: maximum speed 414 mph (666 kmh)
range 2625 miles (4200 km) with external tanks
powerplants two Allison V-1710-111/173 engines
output 2850 hp (2126 kW)

ARMAMENT: one AN-M2 'C' 20 mm cannon and four Colt-Browning 0.50-in machine guns in nose; maximum bomb load of 4000-lb (1814 kg) under wings

FIRST FLIGHT DATE: 27 January 1939 (XP-38)

OPERATOR: USA

PRODUCTION: 2970

From the time of its introduction into combat in mid-1942, the P-38 Lightning was the most successful twin-engined single-seat fighter of World War 2. Its greatest successes were enjoyed in the Pacific and China-Burma-India (CBI) theatres, despite Lockheed's production delivery priorities being granted to USAAF units in Europe in the spirit of the 'Defeat Germany First' policy. There were never more than about 15 squadrons of P-38s in the South and South-west Pacific at any one time, and the CBI boasted only four squadrons, two of which saw most of the action in this remote theatre. The Far East Air Forces (comprising the Fifth and Thirteenth Air Forces) had to make do with just a precious few Lightnings until the advent of the European invasion in mid-1944 released enough of these unique fighters to satisfy operational needs. The speed, range and firepower of the P-38 made it the fighter of choice for most USAAF pilots fighting in the Solomons, New Guinea and the Philippines. Over 1800 Japanese aircraft fell to the guns of P-38s from the Fifth, Seventh and Thirteenth Air Forces in the Pacific and the Tenth and Fourteenth Air Forces in China and Burma, and at war's end Japanese veterans gave grudging tribute to the P-38 as one of their most formidable foes. More than 100 pilots scored at least five aerial victories in the P-38 over the Pacific and CBI, the top American aces of the war flying the aircraft with both confidence and a certain affection which sometimes approached fanatical devotion.

P-38L-5 (serial unknown) of Capt Bob DeHaven, 7th FS/49th FG, Tacloban (Leyte), November 1944

7th FS Ops Executive Bob DeHaven enjoyed himself in the target rich skies over Leyte in the autumn of 1944. He claimed four kills and one damaged between 29 October and 4 November, and all of these victories were almost certainly achieved in this P-38L-5. Quite possibly one of the ex-8th or 475th FG Lightnings hastily commandeered as attrition replacements by the 49th FG in early November, this aircraft was marked with the appropriate blue squadron colours of the 7th FS. And although the fighter did not feature either DeHaven's name or scoreboard beneath the cockpit, someone had still found the time to adorn its twin fins with the 'Screamin' Demons'' Bunyip emblem synonymous with the 7th FS during its spell in Darwin defending northern Australia in 1942. DeHaven's P-38L-5 was reportedly destroyed in an enemy bombing raid soon after its pilot returned home on leave in mid November.

ACE OF ACES

'I opened fire only when the enemy machine filled the entire windscreen. Then, not a single shot missed its mark.'

The most successful fighter pilot in the annals of military aviation, the blond, youthful, almost cherubic-looking Erich Hartmann was credited with a phenomenal 352 enemy aircraft destroyed. The secret of his success lay in a simple, yet highly effective, four-part formula which he had evolved early in his career. He summed it up as 'See – Decide – Attack – Depart'. What he meant by this was gain the advantage of height, await the opportune moment, make one decisive pass at close range and then break off. Hartmann described his formula in the following terms;

'My only tactic was to wait until I had the chance to attack my opponent and then close in at high speed. I opened fire only when the enemy machine filled the entire windscreen. Then, not a single shot missed its mark. The enemy absorbed the full weight of your armament at minimum range and nearly always went down. But whether he did or not, you didn't hang around. If I had only crippled or disabled my opponent I would break off the attack and repeat the process from the beginning.

'To summarise, I would say that in close there is no guesswork. Fly in at full speed, get near enough and you will score. I always began my attacks with the advantage of height if possible. My ideal altitude was 22,000 ft (6700 m). At that height I could best utilise the performance of my aircraft.

'In combat, flying fancy, precision aerobatics are not really of much use. It's the rough manoeuvre which succeeds, throwing the aircraft about violently. I always flew the Bf 109 in combat. The G-model had an excellent rate of climb and handled well in all flight regimes. On the eastern front, the most dangerous enemy

Oberleutnant Erich Hartmann poses for an official photograph soon after being presented with the Diamonds to his Knight's Cross by Adolf Hitler on 26 August 1944. This honour had been bestowed upon him for becoming the first fighter pilot in the world to top the triple century mark (*via John Weal*)

In the month following his promotion to *Staffelkapitän* of 9./JG 52 on 2 September 1943, Leutnant Erich Hartmann regularly flew this near-new Bf 109G-6 in combat over the eastern front (*via John Weal*)

Hauptmann Erich Hartmann is seen here shortly before leaving the famed 'Karaya' *Staffel* on 30 September 1944 to set up the new 4./JG 52 (*via John Weal*)

fighter of them all was the Yak-9, with its heavy engine-mounted cannon.'

And it was a Yak-9 which provided Erich Hartmann with the only one of his 352 kills *not* to be scored with JG 52. For a few days in February 1945 he took over as acting-*Kommandeur* of I./JG 53, based at Veszprem, in Hungary. One of his first actions was to have the unit's aircraft given a coat of dirty grey-white camouflage paint to make them less conspicuous against the snow-covered landscape.

4 February 1945 was a day of intense activity. The *Gruppe* flew at least five missions, most of them *freie Jagd* sweeps against the hordes of Soviet aircraft – La-5s, Yaks, Airacobras, Il-2s – supporting the Red Army's advance through Hungary towards the Austrian border.

Erich Hartmann's wingman on one of these sorties recalls;

'Not long after taking off from Veszprem, we reached the front and saw a formation of about 20 twin-engined Boston bombers with a strong escort of Yak-9s. The *Kommandeur* came on the R/T, giving instructions in plain language to a number of other Bf 109s operating in the area. "Hartmann here – you go after the bombers, I'll take care of the fighters!" after which he immediately attacked and shot down one of the Yak-9s. It was his 337th victory.'

PILOT BIOGRAPHY – ERICH HARTMANN

The son of a physician, Erich Alfred Hartmann was born in Weissach, Württemberg, on 19 April 1922. Following in his father's footsteps, he intended to study medicine had the war not intervened. Instead, he left school at the age of 18 in September 1940 and joined the Luftwaffe the following month.

Hartmann was two years in training, spending time at both the cadet college in Berlin and the fighter school at Zerbst, before joining his first operational unit – 7. *Staffel* of JG 52 – at Soldatskaya, on the southern sector of the eastern front, in October 1942. His first victory – an Il-2 – was achieved over the Caucasus on 5 November 1942, but it would be nearly three months (27 January 1943) before he doubled his tally by downing a MiG-1 fighter. Although something of a slow starter, Hartmann claimed his first double – a brace of LaGG-3s – on 30 April 1943 to take his score into double figures. Six months later almost to the day, on 29 October 1943, Leutnant Erich Hartmann was awarded the Knight's Cross for a total of 148 kills! His star was very much in the ascendent, and multiple daily victories had become commonplace. By this time he had been appointed *Kapitän* of 9./JG 52, the famous 'Karaya' *Staffel*.

The Oak Leaves followed on 2 March 1944 for his reaching a total of 200, and the Swords on 4 July – three days after Hartmann's promotion to Oberleutnant – for 239. On 18 July he became only the fourth pilot to achieve 250 victories, and his eleven kills on 24 August took his score to 301. The first pilot in the world to be credited with a triple century, this feat earned Hartmann the Diamonds the following day. Promoted to Hauptmann on 1 September 1944, he duly took over as *Staffelkapitän* of the reformed 4./JG 52 a month later, and also served as acting *Kommandeur* of II. *Gruppe* Invited to join Adolf Galland's Me 262-equipped JV 44, Hartmann declined, preferring instead to return to JG 52 on the eastern front for the remaining weeks of the war, which he saw out as *Kommandeur* of I. *Gruppe*. On 8 May 1945 – the day hostilities ceased in Europe – Erich Hartmann scored his 352nd, and last kill, and was promoted to Major.

Despite surrendering his unit to the US Third Army, Hartmann was handed over to Soviet troops and subsequently spent the next ten years in a series of prison camps, where he endured innumerable hardships. In 1955 he at last returned home to his wife, and joined the newly-formed West German air force. He remained with the new Luftwaffe until 1970, when he retired with the rank of Oberst. Subsequently joining the Federal Aviation Authority, Hartmann also managed several flying schools in the Wurttemberg area. Opting for full retirement in the late 1980s, he passed away on 19 Setpember 1993.

Bf 109G-6 'White 1' of Hauptmann Erich Hartmann, *Staffelkapitän* 4./JG 52, Budaörs, Hungary, November 1944

Erich Hartmann positively advertised his presence in the air, being known to the Russians as the 'Black Devil of the South'. This is the late model G-6 flown by him after he relinquished his year-long command of 9. *Staffel* to set up a new 4./JG 52 in October 1944. Although the machine retains the distinctive black 'tulip-leaf' which was Hartmann's individual marking, the 'Karaya' *Staffel's* famous 'pierced heart' emblem below the cockpit is now a plain red heart bearing the name *'Usch'* (for Ursula, whom Hartmann had married two months previously). Note, however, there is no record of the ace's current score, which by this time was well above the 300 mark.

SPECIFICATION

Messerschmitt Bf 109G/K
(all dimensions and performance data for Bf 109G-6)

TYPE:	single-engined monoplane fighter
ACCOMMODATION:	pilot
DIMENSIONS:	length 29 ft 7.5 in (9.03 m) wingspan 32 ft 6.5 in (9.92 m) height 8 ft 2.5 in (2.50 m)
WEIGHTS:	empty 5893 lb (2673 kg) maximum take-off 7496 lb (3400 kg)
PERFORMANCE:	maximum speed 386 mph (621 kmh) range 620 miles (998 km) with external tank powerplant Daimler-Benz DB 605AM output 1800 hp (1342 kW)
ARMAMENT:	one Rheinmetall Borsig MK 108 20 mm cannon in propeller hub and two Rheinmetall Borsig MG 131 13 mm machine guns in upper cowling, two Mauser MG 151 20 mm cannon in underwing gondolas; provision for various underfuselage and underwing stores
FIRST FLIGHT DATE:	late summer 1941
OPERATORS:	Bulgaria, Croatia, Finland, Germany, Hungary, Italy, Rumania, Slovakia, Switzerland, Spain
PRODUCTION:	approximately 24,000 G-models and around 750 K-models

The highest-scoring aces in the history of aerial conflict were the *Jagdwaffe* pilots involved in the bloody combats on the eastern front from June 1941 through to May 1945. Men like Erich Hartmann (352 kills), Gerhard Barkhorn (301 kills) and Günther Rall (275 kills) all scored the bulk of their staggering victory tallies against the massed ranks of the Soviet Red Air Forces, with a further seven German pilots all passing the 200-mark during the campaign. The most common fighter used by these pilots was the venerable Bf 109, which was involved in the action from Operation *Barbarossa* through to the climactic Battle for Berlin in the spring of 1945. Units such as JGs 51, 52 and 54 all flew the Messerschmitt fighter in the east, progressing from the *Emil* to the final versions of the *Gustav*. Although the continual addition of weighty items such as wing cannon and larger engines to the once slight airframe of the Bf 109 had adversely affected the fighter's legendary manoeuvrability by 1943-44, the late-build G-10/14 and Bf 109K-4 were still more than a match for the latest generation of Soviet fighters at the medium to low altitudes at which most aerial action took place in the east.

'WHITE 27'

'With uncontrolled agitation, I open fire, and the Messerschmitt 262 literally falls apart and pieces tumble earthwards.'

On 19 February 1945, 176 GIAP's Ivan Kozhedub and his wingman, Dmitrii Titarenko, were 'free hunting' near the frontline. Flying south of Frankfurt at an altitude of some 3500 metres, they spotted an aircraft following the River Oder at a speed equal to the maximum performance of their Lavochkin La-7 fighters – one of the fastest piston-engined machines of World War 2. Their foe was evidently an Me 262 jet fighter. Kozhedub whipped his aircraft around and set off in pursuit at full speed. The pilot of the Messerschmitt seemed to be unaware of the danger behind him, trusting in the unrivalled performance of his aircraft, and thus neglecting to check his tail. Wringing every bit of speed from his machine, Kozhedub gradually closed the distance and tried to manoeuvre behind and slightly below the Me 262 so that he might at least get a good look at it, if not also open fire. Meanwhile, he summoned Titarenko. 'Dima, don't delay!'

Both Kozhedub and his wingman were thoroughly familiar with the existence of the Messerschmitt fighter, as the ranking Soviet ace revealed in the following post-war account of this engagement;

'We had learned from intelligence reports that individual examples of aircraft powered by turbojet engines had been spotted – these were, of course, Messerschmitt 262s. They could remain in the air much longer than the rocket-powered Messerschmitt 163 "flying wings" that we had also read about. The new Messerschmitt posed a serious threat to be reckoned with. They had been seen both on the ground and in the air. Their speed was higher than the speed of our propeller aircraft, although their manoeuvrability was poorer. They attempted to attack our *Shturmoviks* and bombers and then quickly vanished. They even conducted ground attacks on our forces.

Proudly wearing his Hero of the Soviet Union (HSU) star and other medals, Ivan Kozhedub emerges from the cockpit of his La-5FN, which had been donated by Vasilii Konev. This photograph was taken in Moldavia in the late spring of 1944 (*via Carl-Fredrik Geust*)

'Tactics for fighting them had still not been developed, but we had been advised that the most important thing was to observe the Messerschmitt 262, and if a suitable chance presented itself, to attack it with the goal of testing the combat capabilities of our machines.

'On 19 February 1945, Dmitrii Titarenko and I had a meeting with a fascist jet aircraft. Flying along the Oder at the maximum speed of our Lavochkins, I soon realise that this must be a jet aircraft! Quickly whipping around, I give my fighter full throttle and head off in pursuit of the enemy. I approach his tail, getting to within 500 metres of the jet. A successful manoeuvre, agility and speed have allowed me to approach my quarry.

'But what's this? Tracers fly at him – it is clear that my wingman was over-eager! I angrily curse Titarenko under my breath, for I am certain that my plan of action had now been irretrievably ruined. But his tracers unexpectedly help me, as the German pilot begins to turn to the left – in my direction. The distance sharply narrows and I close with the enemy. With uncontrolled agitation, I open fire, and the Messerschmitt 262 literally falls apart and pieces tumble earthwards.'

Kozhedub, who had just claimed kill number 58, later discovered that the pilot of the Messerschmitt fighter was Unteroffizier Kurt Lange of 1./KG(J) 54.

The donation La-5FN serving as a backdrop to this photograph of Ivan Kozhedub was presented to him on 2 May 1944. Upon his transfer from 240 IAP to 176 GIAP, the fighter was handed over to Kozhedub's deputy, Pavel Bryzgalov, who flew it until October. Fellow ace Kirill Evstigneev then acquired the veteran fighter following a spell in hospital recuperating from wounds. The inscription on the fighter's seldom photographed port side read 'In the name of Hero of the Soviet Union Podpolkovnik (Lt Col) Konev, N'. On the right side was the inscription 'From the kolkhoznik (collective farmer) Konev, Vasilii Viktorovich'. This aeroplane was paid for with funds raised by Vasilii Konev in honour of his relative, Lt Col Konev, who had perished in the fighting on the western borders in 1941, and who had purportedly been awarded the HSU. Strangely, no such Lt Col N Konev can be found in the official lists of HSU recipients (via Carl-Fredrik Geust)

Ivan Kozhedub flew La-7 'White 27' during his time as Deputy CO of 176 GIAP, which commenced in August 1944 and lasted until war's end. The aircraft was preserved after the conflict, and is seen here on display in the late 1960s. The fighter is marked with its famous pilot's triple Gold Stars of the HSU and his full tally of 62 kills. The aircraft presently resides in the Air Force Museum at Monino (via Carl-Fredrik Geust)

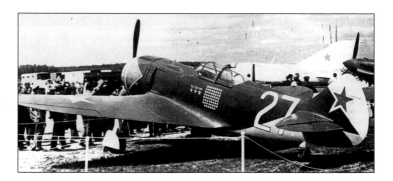

PILOT BIOGRAPHY – IVAN KOZHEDUB

Ivan Kozhedub was the top-scoring Allied ace of World War 2, and a three-time Hero of the Soviet Union (HSU).

Born on 8 June 1920 in Obrazhievka, in the Sumy region of the USSR, Kozhedub learned to fly with the Shostkinsk aeroclub pre-war. He joined the army in 1940, and graduated from the Chuguyevsk Military Air School in February of the following year. Fortunate enough to be retained as a flight instructor, and thus avoiding the wholesale slaughter of his contemporaries at the hands of the Luftwaffe in the wake of the German invasion in June 1941, Kozhedub was posted to 240 IAP at his own request in March 1943 – this unit had been one of the first to be equipped with the new La-5.

Kozhedub was almost shot down by a Bf 110 on his first mission, and it took him some 40 sorties before he scored his first kill (a Ju 87) on 6 July 1943. By now flying the more advanced La-5F, he started to claim victories on a more regular basis, and he soon became a squadron commander. On 4 February 1944, Kozhedub was awarded his first HSU with his score standing at 26 victories – he was also promoted to captain. In early May Kozhedub was given a special presentation La-5FN which had been donated by collective farmer Vasilii Konev. The ace duly claimed eight victories with the machine in the spring and summer of 1944.

In late June Kozhedub was ordered to fly immediately to Moscow, having by then completed 256 sorties and scored 48 victories. There, he was informed that he was being transferred as deputy commander to a regiment assigned to be 'free hunt' specialists. Kozhedub spent August retraining on the new La-7, and on the 19th of the month he received his second HSU. Three days later he was given a factory-fresh La-7 and sent to his new regiment, which had just been designated 176 Guards IAP. Within weeks Kozhedub had been promoted to major.

By war's end the ranking Soviet ace had flown 330 sorties and scored 62 official individual victories. He claimed that he had actually shot down more than 100 aircraft, but many remained unconfirmed because they were destroyed deep within enemy territory. He also never bothered counting his group kills. Amongst his victories was an Me 262 shot down in February 1945 – one of just six jet kills claimed by Soviet pilots. Kozhedub received his third HSU on 18 August 1945, an award equalled only by Marshal Zhukov and Aleksandr Pokryshkin.

From March 1951 to February 1952, Kozhedub commanded the MiG-15-equipped 324 IAD in combat over North Korea, although he was forbidden by Stalin himself from undertaking combat missions. Kozhedub continued flying fighters until 1970. Retiring from active duty in 1978 with the rank of Marshal, he died on 8 August 1991.

La-7 'White 27' of Maj Ivan Kozhedub, 176 GIAP, Germany, late April 1945
Kozhedub was issued with this La-7 in August 1944, and he took it with him to 176 GIAP that same month. The fighter arrived in the frontline with solid grey uppersurfaces and light blue undersides, to which a regimental red nose and white tail markings were added. Kozhedub initially had 48 kills and two HSU stars marked beneath the cockpit, but by the time Berlin fell his tally of victory stars had increased to 62. A third HSU star would also be added on 18 August 1945.

SPECIFICATION

Lavochkin La-5/-7

(all dimensions and performance data for La-7)

TYPE:	single-engined monoplane fighter
ACCOMMODATION:	pilot
DIMENSIONS:	length 29 ft 2.5 in (8.90 m) wingspan 32 ft 1.75 in (9.80 m) height 8 ft 6.25 in (2.60 m)
WEIGHTS:	empty 5842 lb (2620 kg) maximum take-off 7496 lb (3400 kg)
PERFORMANCE:	maximum speed 423 mph (680 kmh) range 615 miles (990 km) powerplant Shvetsov M-82FN output 1850 hp (1380 kW)
ARMAMENT:	two or three Shpital'ny-Vladimirov 20 mm cannon in upper cowling; provision for bombs or rockets under wings
FIRST FLIGHT DATE:	March 1942 (La-5)
OPERATORS:	Czechoslovakia, USSR
PRODUCTION:	9920 La-5s and 5753 La-7s

Reports of the LaGG-3's inadequacies in combat against Luftwaffe (and Finnish) fighters resulted in the aircraft's inline M-105PF being replaced by the more powerful Shvetsov M-82 radial in early 1942. Testing soon proved that the modified fighter was not only appreciably faster than its predecessor, but also far more capable at medium to high altitudes. Designated the Lavochkin La-5, the first examples to reach the frontline (during the battle for Stalingrad in late 1942) were actually re-engined LaGG-3s. Aside from the change of powerplant, the aircraft had also had its machine gun armament replaced by two 20 mm cannon. By late March 1943 production of the definitive La-5N had commenced, this variant featuring a fuel-injected M-82FN for better performance at altitude and cut down rear fuselage decking and a new canopy for better all round vision. The La-5FN was more than a match for the Bf 109G, and could hold its own with the Fw 190. In November 1943 the further improved La-7 started flight trials, this model boasting even greater performance thanks to the lightening of its overall structure and adoption of the metal wing spars featured in late-build La-5FNs. Attention was also paid to reducing the fighter's drag coefficient, which resulted in the fitment of inboard wing leading edge surfaces and a revised cowling. The La-7 entered service in the spring of 1944, and went on to become the favoured mount of most Soviet aces.

'KING OF THE STRAFERS'

'This is "Windsor". I'm hit bad, oil pressure dropping. I can't make it back. I have got enough ammo for one more pass.'

'See you in a few days', were the last known words of one of the Eighth Air Force's most respected fighter leaders, and its leading strafing ace. But Lt Col Elwyn Righetti was never to be seen again by his compatriots after he crash-landed his flak-damaged P-51D following an attack on a Luftwaffe airfield on 17 April 1945.

The 55th FG, led by Righetti, had escorted bombers from the 3rd Air Division to Dresden prior to leaving the 'heavies' and searching out targets on the ground to strafe. The weather was bad, but towards the end of the mission the Mustangs were able to drop through the overcast and catch some Fw 190s taking off from fields in the area. Nine were downed before the strafing began. Righetti led his pilots in an attack on Riesa/Canitz airfield, near Breslau, in Germany, where Fw 190s and Bf 109s were spotted.

Capt Carroll Henry was flying on Righetti's wing as they went through a hole in the clouds and prepared to test the flak defences of Riesa/Canitz, which appeared full of parked aircraft. Just as Henry was about to make his first pass, Righetti told him to take care of an Fw 190 which was preparing to land. While the colonel made his attack on the airfield, Henry downed the Fw 190. He later reported;

'When I had destroyed the '190, I took a quick look at the field to locate the colonel, before making any passes myself. I observed fires from three Me 109s at this time. I made a pass from north to south on a large dispersal area northeast of the airfield. I got in a two-

A vastly experienced pilot by the time he arrived in the ETO in the autumn of 1944, Lt Col Elwyn Righetti had spent the previous four years instructing future fighter pilots (*via William Hess*)

Lt Col Elwyn Righetti and his personal aircraft, P-51D 44-14223 *KATYDID*, pose in the snow at Wormingford in January 1945. From its general appearance, it is obvious that this aircraft had seen a lot of action during the winter of 1944-45 (*via William Hess*)

A rare photograph of Lt Col Elwyn Righetti, the 'king of the strafers' and CO of the 55th FG in the final months of the war. His score of 27 destroyed on the ground was unsurpassed, and his reputation was further enhanced by 7.5 aerial victories. But he did not survive to enjoy his fame, failing to return from an airfield strafing mission on 17 April 1945. Note the elaborate and artistically-rendered swastikas to the left of Righetti (*via William Hess*)

second burst at an unidentified single-engined aircraft and saw it burst into flames. I pulled up and saw Col Righetti making a strafing pass, his aeroplane streaming coolant. He now had seven fires burning.

'He called over the R/T, "This is 'Windsor'. I'm hit bad, oil pressure dropping. I can't make it back. I have got enough ammo for one more pass". I watched him make that pass and obtain good hits on two more aircraft. I could not watch for fires as I wanted to give the colonel cover on any move he might make. After his pass, he pulled up slightly and levelled off on a course of 270 degrees, flying about five miles before belly-landing in an open field. After he was on the ground I received the following message over the R/T. "I broke my nose but I'm okay. I got nine today. Tell my family I'm okay. It has been swell working with you gang. Be seeing you shortly".'

The nine aircraft destroyed would take Lt Col Righetti's final score to 7.5 aerial and 27 strafing kills. But there would be no reunion, for he was never heard from again. It was assumed that Righetti met his death at the hands of angry civilians. He was one of five 55th FG pilots who did not return that day, and only one would subsequently emerge from a PoW camp post-war.

PILOT BIOGRAPHY – ELWYN RIGHETTI

Elwyn Righetti was born on 17 April 1915 in San Luis Obispo, California. He had initially learned to fly in the Civilian Pilot Training Program after attending California Poly Tech. Righetti then joined the Army Air Corps in November 1939 and graduated from pilot training at Kelly Field, Texas, on 25 July 1940. Although he repeatedly requested a transfer to combat, he was not released from Training Command until he had reached the rank of lieutenant colonel in October 1944. Leaving his post as commander of the Advanced Instructor Training Unit at Randolph Field in October 1944, Righetti was assigned to the Eighth Air Force's 55th FG and made CO of the group's 338th FS at Wormingford, in Essex.

He shared a victory over a Bf 109 on 2 November 1944, and on Christmas Eve downed three Fw 190s. Righetti destroyed another Bf 109 on 13 January 1945, and on 3 February he intercepted some unusual adversaries – *Mistel* combinations, comprising explosive-laden Junkers Ju 88s with Fw 190s attached to provide guidance to the target. Righetti quickly downed two *Mistels* to 'make ace'.

Righetti was also an enthusiastic strafer, and by the beginning of April 1945 he had destroyed six aircraft on the ground. During the course of that month his attacks on aircraft at various German airfields across northern Europe were to become the stuff of legend. He destroyed six aircraft on the 9th and another six on the 16th. The next day, on his final mission, Righetti destroyed nine enemy aircraft before he had to belly land his Mustang when its coolant system was damaged by flak. Afterwards, he radioed that he was okay, and would see his fellow pilots in a few days. This was not to be. He was never seen again, and it has been speculated that he fell victim to attack by German civilians. Righetti's final tally was 7.5 aerial and 27 strafing victories.

P-51D-10 44-14223 *KATYDID* of Lt Col Elwyn Righetti, 55th FG, Wormingford, March 1945

'King of the strafers', Lt Col Righetti flew this machine for much of his brief time in the ETO. The aircraft saw extensive use with the 55th FG, flying both bomber escort and strafing sorties. Righetti took the machine with him when he was promoted from 338th FS CO to commander of the 55th FG on 22 February 1945. Almost certainly used by the ace to claim all 7.5 of his aerial victories, 44-14223 was replaced by brand new P-51D-20 44-72227 in early April. Also coded CL-M, and named *KATYDID*, this machine was shot down by flak during an airfield attack on Riesa/Canitz airfield, near Breslau in Germany, on 17 April 1945.

SPECIFICATION

North American P-51D/K Mustang

TYPE:	single-engined monoplane fighter
ACCOMMODATION:	pilot
DIMENSIONS:	length 32 ft 3 in (9.83 m) wingspan 37 ft 0 in (11.28 m) height 12 ft 2 in (3.71 m)
WEIGHTS:	empty 7635 lb (3463 kg) maximum take-off 12,100 lb (5488 kg)
PERFORMANCE:	maximum speed 437 mph (703 kmh) range 1650 miles (2655 km) with external tanks powerplant Packard V-1650-7 output 1720 hp (1283 kW)
ARMAMENT:	six Colt-Browning 0.50-in machine guns in wings; up to 2000-lb (907 kg) of bombs or six 5-in (12.7 cm) rocket projectiles under wings
FIRST FLIGHT DATE:	17 November 1943
OPERATORS:	Australia, China, South Africa, UK, USA
PRODUCTION:	9493

The P-51D was effectively an improved version of the B/C-model Mustang that had first been fitted with the Merlin 61 engine in late 1942. One of the major complaints from Eighth Air Force fighter pilots who debuted the revised Mustang in combat in early 1944 centred on the poor rearward visibility on offer. North American Aviation quickly set about rectifying this with the follow-on P-51D, which was designed from the outset to feature a cut-down rear fuselage and a 360-degree clear vision tear-drop canopy. The new variant also boasted an additional two 0.50-in machine guns in the wings, although the engine remained the same as was installed in late-production P-51B/Cs – the licence-produced Packard V-1650-7. The first D-model Mustangs arrived in the ETO just prior to D-Day, and the aircraft had replaced all 'razorback' P-51s in-theatre by year-end. Despite its better visibility and improved armament, the newer model was not universally welcomed by all, as Lt Elmer O'Dell of the 363rd FG explained; 'I flew all of my missions in the same P-51B-10, and in June 1944 I was offered a P-51D, but I preferred to keep the B-10. I checked out the D and flew a number of mock combat missions in it, but to me it didn't have the delicate response of the B-10, which had four 0.50-calibre guns. When they built the D they added another gun to each wing. To do so, they had to alter the configuration of the wing. I maintain this caused a small reduction in manoeuvrability. I guess it was a personal thing, for obviously most pilots thought otherwise'.

KATYDID

FINAL VICTORY

'They approached undetected and attacked, Bencetic firing from a distance of 260 ft. Hitting the Mustang's radiator and wings, he succeeded in setting the RAF fighter on fire.'

Ljudevit 'Lujo' Bencetic is seen in the German Alps in early 1943 (*via Boris Ciglic*)

Around midday on 23 April 1945, the commanding officer of 2. *Lovacko Jato* ZNDH, satnik Ljudevit Bencetic (flying Bf 109G-10 'Black 22'), together with his wingman, porucnik Mihajlo Jelak (in Bf 109G-14 'Black 27'), were returning to Lucko airfield after an uneventful patrol when, east of Zagreb, they spotted two RAF Mustangs IVs of No 213 Sqn below them. Although Croat pilots generally avoided combat with Allied aircraft at this late stage of the war, this was an opportunity too good to be missed. They approached undetected and attacked, Bencetic firing from a distance of 260 ft (80 m). Hitting the Mustang's radiator and wings, he succeeded in setting the RAF fighter on fire. Flg Off Francis J Barrett, flying Mustang Mk IVA KH869, tried to escape, but Bencetic's second burst from an even shorter distance tore into his aircraft's fuselage and he crashed fatally in the Turopolje area.

In the meantime, Jelak had attacked the second British fighter, and he claimed to have shot it down prior to two more Mustangs appearing on the scene and forcing him to crash-land near Velika Gorica, close to the Zagreb-Sisak railway line. In reality, there were four No 213 Sqn aircraft in the area, but only one pair became involved with the Croats, and Jelak was actually a victim of the

pilot he was thought to have shot down, Flt Lt Graham Hulse, who was flying Mustang Mk IVA KH826. Hulse duly claimed a Bf 109 damaged in the Okucani-Zagreb area. The whole combat lasted some ten minutes at different heights, starting at 6500 ft (2000 m) and descending down to treetop height. Bencetic's 16th confirmed kill was also the last aerial victory achieved by a Croatian pilot in World War 2.

Having fought the Red Air Force for much of World War 2, the *Zrakoplovstvo Nezavisne Drzave Hrvatske* (ZNDH) only entered combat with the RAF's Balkan Air Force in the final weeks of the war. On 24 March 1945, vod Asim Korhut and vod Ivan Mihaljevic were attacked by five Spitfires VIIIs (probably from No 73 Sqn) between Sisak and Petrinja, although they managed to escape. Both Mihaljevic and his Bf 109G-14 had been hit in the clash, however, and he force-landed near the village of Hrastovice. He died from his wounds before help could arrive. That same day, eight RAF Mustangs of Nos 213 and 249 Sqns attacked Lucko airfield using napalm bombs. One No 213 Sqn aircraft was

brought down by flak, and although the returning pilots claimed two Fw 190s and one Ju 88 destroyed, plus one unidentified aircraft damaged, on the ground, their actual score was far higher. The ZNDH had lost three Bf 109s and one MS 406 destroyed and the Luftwaffe an Fw 190. In addition, three ZNDH Bf 109s, three G.50s and a single Bf 108, Bf 110 and MS 406 had been damaged, as had two Fw 190s, one Ju 88 and several Bf 109s and Hs 126s of the Luftwaffe.

On 30 March four *Gustavs* escorted a similar number of Do 17s attacking 4.JA partisan army positions near Gospic. The RAF duly scrambled Spitfires from No 73 Sqn, and two Do 17s were shot down, although the Croat fighters escaped into the clouds, with only the Bf 109G-14 of vod Antun Plese being slightly damaged.

There were further clashes with RAF Spitfires on 2 April, when four *Gustavs* were sent to attack partisan forces near the village of Medak. The first pair, comprising Bencetic and Jelak, made one strafing pass and left, but the second was intercepted by No 73 Sqn Spitfire Mk IXs. Canadian Plt Off Norman John Pearce shot down the leading aircraft, which crash-landed in no-man's land near Primislje. The final action between the RAF and the ZNDH took place on 23 April 1945, as depicted in the artwork featured in this chapter.

Bf 109G-2 'Yellow 12' of 15(*Kroat*)./JG 52 is prepared for its next sortie out in the open at Kertch in the spring of 1943. Fifteen-kill ace Ljudevit Bencetic claimed a Yak-1 while flying this aircraft on 6 May 1943 (*via Boris Ciglic*)

Marked with the distinctive 'Zvonimir' cross, Bf 109G-14AS 'Black 17' of 2.LJ is kept locked away in a hangar at Lucko airfield in the spring of 1945. Yugoslav Army units found nine ZNDH, Luftwaffe and *Magyar Kiralyi Honved Legiero* (Hungarian) *Gustavs* at Lucko following the surrender of Axis forces in the area (*via Boris Ciglic*)

PILOT BIOGRAPHY – LJUDEVIT BENCETIC

Born on 26 December 1910 in Zagreb, Bencetic graduated from 7.VP (aviation regiment) in Mostar in 1930 and became a military pilot in 1932. He was promoted to nizi vojno-tehnicki cinovnik III klase (equivalent to porucnik, or lieutenant) in December 1940.

The outbreak of war found Bencetic fulfilling a non-flying role with 12. *Bazna Ceta Vazduhoplovnog Zavoda* (base company of air force arsenal) in Kraljevo. He joined the ZNDH in May 1941, and transferred to the HZL (*Hrvatska Zrakoplovna Legija*) in July with the rank of nadporucnik. During his first combat tour Bencetic scored 14 confirmed victories and one unconfirmed kill. He added one confirmed and one unconfirmed kill during his second tour. By the end of 1943 Bencetic had flown a total of 250 missions, and had also served as an instructor with JG 104 at Fürth between July and September of that year.

Later employed on ferry duties with *Flugzeugüberführungs Geschwader* 1 at Wiener Neustadt, before being put in command of 3/*Kroatien Jagdgruppe* 1 (later renamed 3/JGr Kro) in December, Bencetic was promoted to satnik the following February. In September 1944, following the disbanding of most HZL units, he moved to 5. *Zrakoplovna Luka* (air base) Zaluaeani to command its MS 406-equipped 14.LJ. Bencetic flew three combat missions against the NOVJ (*Narodnooslobodilacki Vojska Jugoslavije*) and then engaged in ground battles with advancing partisan forces.

Given command of 13. *Zrakoplovno Jato* (air squadron) at Bjelovar airfield, Bencetic was made CO of Borongaj-based 2.LJ in November 1944. He became the last Croatian pilot to claim an aerial victory in World War 2 when he downed a RAF Mustang on 23 April 1945 east of Zagreb. Bencetic then escaped to Austria, but was returned by the British to face a court martial in Zagreb. Granted amnesty in July 1945, he moved to Germany, where his wife, ex-Luftwaffe helferin Hella Stampa, awaited him. Ljudevit Bencetic duly changed his name to Ludwig Stampa and died in the late 1980s in Mainz Kastel.

SPECIFICATION

Messerschmitt Bf 109G/K

(all dimensions and performance data for Bf 109G-6)

TYPE:	single-engined monoplane fighter
ACCOMMODATION:	pilot
DIMENSIONS:	length 29 ft 7.5 in (9.03 m) wingspan 32 ft 6.5 in (9.92 m) height 8 ft 2.5 in (2.50 m)
WEIGHTS:	empty 5893 lb (2673 kg) maximum take-off 7496 lb (3400 kg)
PERFORMANCE:	maximum speed 386 mph (621 kmh) range 620 miles (998 km) with external tank powerplant Daimler-Benz DB 605AM output 1800 hp (1342 kW)
ARMAMENT:	one Rheinmetall Borsig MK 108 20 mm cannon in propeller hub and two Rheinmetall Borsig MG 131 13 mm machine guns in upper cowling, two Mauser MG 151 20 mm cannon in underwing gondolas; provision for various underfuselage and underwing stores
FIRST FLIGHT DATE:	late summer 1941
OPERATORS:	Bulgaria, Croatia, Finland, Germany, Hungary, Italy, Rumania, Slovakia, Switzerland, Spain
PRODUCTION:	approximately 24,000 G-models and around 750 K-models

The Bf 109 was the principal fighter of the Royal Yugoslav Air Force prior to the Axis invasion in April 1941, and the Air Force of the Independent State of Croatia following the creation of the pro-German state in the Balkans in the wake of the occupation. Some 83 Bf 109E-3as had been supplied to the Yugoslavs in the latter half of 1939, and these formed the backbone of the air force's modest fighter arm. The *Emils* saw combat against German and Italian aircraft when Yugoslavia was invaded on 6 April 1941, pilots scoring a number of victories over Axis types, although at some cost. The surviving aircraft were used by the newly-formed ZNDH, while more *Emils* and a handful of F-models were supplied to the Croatian Air Force Legion by the Germans for use on the eastern front in the autumn of 1941. The Legion's squadrons were effectively Luftwaffe units, its aircraft wearing full German markings and its crews German uniforms and insignia. Assigned to 15(*Kroat*)./JG 52, the Croatian unit remained equipped with Bf 109E-3/4s until July 1942, when it re-equipped with Bf 109G-2s. Croatian fighter pilots continued to fight the Red Air Force until returning home to defend their country in late 1944. Small numbers of late-build Bf 109G-14s and K-4s continued to be supplied to the Croats right up until the final two weeks of the war. By then, Messerschmitt fighters were flying with both Axis-aligned forces and the newly-formed Yugoslav Air Force.

Bf 109G-10 'Black 4' (2104), 2.LJ, Lucko, March 1945

This aircraft wears the ZNDH markings that were introduced in the final weeks of the war in Europe. The machine also features full yellow theatre markings, as well as the 2.LJ emblem beneath the cockpit. Seeing limited action in Croatia in February and March 1945, this aircraft was used by Slovakian pilot Vladimir Sandtner to defect to Falconara, in Italy, on 16 April.

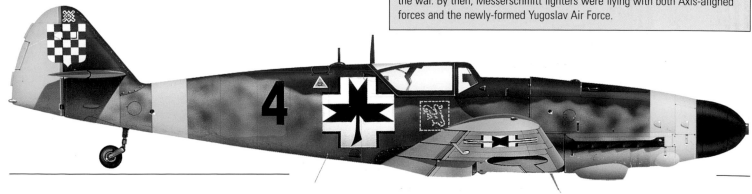

MiG MAULER

'I saw the armour-piercing incendiaries hit his fuselage and left wing. He did two violent snap rolls and started to spin.'

The 334th FIS's Capt James Jabara gets a victory ride from two fellow 4th FIG Sabre pilots upon his return to Suwon after becoming the first American jet ace on 20 May 1951 (*USAF*)

On 26 May 1953, second-ranking USAF Korean War ace Maj James Jabara went head-to-head with a formation of 16 MiG-15s at high altitude over Uiju. He was leading a formation of four F-86F Sabres from the 334th FIS/4th FIG on a patrol along 'MiG Alley' at the time, the ace spotting the large communist formation across the Yalu River. Without hesitating, he immediately engaged the MiGs head-on, scattering the silver fighters all over the sky. Jabara claimed two kills following this mission – one jet shot down and the other forced into an uncontrollable flick roll when its pilot tried to evade Jabara's aggressive collision course attack. These were the American's eight and ninth victories of the war.

One year earlier, on 20 May 1951, veteran fighter pilot Jabara had earned the distinction of being the first all-jet ace of the USAF. His combat report for this historic mission read as follows;

'We found about a half-dozen MiGs coming in on us. Another pair of Sabres split the enemy formation and we tacked onto the other three. I was just setting up for a firing position when three more MiGs attacked us. They overshot me as I turned into them. Two broke away, but I latched onto the tail of the third one. He tried everything in the book to shake me but he couldn't. I closed to within 1500 ft and gave him three good bursts. I saw the armour-piercing incendiaries hit his fuselage and left wing. He did two violent snap rolls and started to spin. At 10,000 ft, with my wingman and I circling him, the MiG pilot bailed out. It was a good thing for him that he didn't wait any longer because the MiG exploded a few seconds later.

'The next few minutes were wild, with 28 Sabres trying to watch some 50 MiGs buzzing around them like angry bees.

I climbed back up to 20,000 ft and spotted six more MiGs. I was in a good position so I bounced them. Picking one of them out, I closed the range and got off two good bursts, scoring heavily both times on his fuselage and tail surfaces. He flamed out right away, with smoke pouring from his exhaust. One more bullet hit him right in the middle and he caught fire.

'Quickly I cut my power and popped the speed brakes, following him down to about 6500 ft to make sure that he hit the ground. All of a sudden I heard a "popcorn machine" right in my cockpit. Looking back, I saw two MiGs firing at me, and they had a very good position. My wingman should have warned me, but he had been busy with some other MiGs while I was attacking these. I was in big trouble.

'Breaking left, I went to full throttle and closed the brakes. For about two minutes we were all over the sky, with them shooting

Capt Jabara conducts an interview at Suwon in front of the camera soon after 'making ace' on 20 May 1951. Behind him is the aircraft he used to claim these victories, F-86A-5 49-1318, which has clearly been cleaned up for the benefit of the camera – there is no muzzle soot around the gun ports. Although its pilot was removed from the frontline with immediate effect after the 20 May mission, this historic machine remained at Suwon and was eventually written off on 2 January 1952 in an unspecified incident. It was one of 12 Sabres lost by the USAF that month in Korea (*via Warren Thompson*)

all the time and me running like hell, and doing some jinks and things that the F-86 wasn't meant to do. Then I heard two other guys from my flight on the R/T. "There's an F-86 in trouble down there!" I came right on with, "Roger, I know it only too damned well!" "Call us if you need help!", they said. Since I was on "Bingo Fuel", I said, "I sure could use some!"

'The two F-86s rolled over and came down to my aid. They were just beautiful! One MiG, seeing help on the way, broke off and ran for home. The other MiG held on and kept firing. Gene Holley was one of the F-86 drivers. He pulled in behind the MiG and started to pour fire into him. We flew round and round, me running, the MiG firing at me, Holley firing at him, and Pitts, in the other F-86, covering all of us. The MiG started to smoke and broke off his attack, heading back across the Yalu. Since we were below "bingo", none of us could give chase. I called Holley. "Thanks for saving my neck!" It had been a very rough 20 minutes.'

Having upheld the reputation of the 4th FIG – proudly emblazoned on the sign above them at Kimpo – over the Yalu on 26 May 1953, Maj James Jabara (two kills) and 1Lts William Mailloux (one kill) and Richard W Frailey (one kill) pose for the camera. These victories took Jabara's tally to nine (*USAF*)

PILOT BIOGRAPHY – JAMES JABARA

James Jabara was born in Muskogee, Oklahoma, on 10 October 1923. During his school years his family moved to Kansas, and he graduated from Wichita High School in May 1942. His interest in aviation dated back to his formative years, when barnstorming was in its prime, but only 5 ft 5in in height, and with poor eyesight, Jabara's dream of becoming a fighter pilot seemed almost impossible. Rumour has it that he consumed heavy doses of Vitamin A to improve his sight, and this apparently worked well enough for him to be accepted into the USAAF's pilot training programme right out of high school. He received his wings on 1 October 1943 and was posted to the Ninth Air Force's 382nd FS/363rd FG in England in April 1944.

Flying P-51B/Ds with the group, he claimed 1.5 aerial kills prior to returning home tour-expired in August. Jabara returned to England in February 1945 when he was posted to the 354th FS/355th FG, and he remained with the unit until war's end – by which time he had flown more than 100 missions. Staying in the air force post-war, Jabara attended Tactical Air School at Tyndall air force base and then completed a tour in Okinawa with the 53rd FG. He transitioned to the F-86A in 1950 and was posted to the 334th FIS/4th FIG. Jabara went to Korea with the unit in December 1950, and on 20 May 1951 he downed his fifth and sixth MiG-15s to become the first American jet ace. Jabara was immediately withdrawn from Korea and flown to Japan the very next day, senior USAF officers deeming the first jet ace too valuable to risk in combat.

Finally managing to get reassigned to the 4th FIG in January 1953, Jabara once again made an impact in the skies over Korea. By this stage of the war close to 800 MiG-15s were based north of the Yalu in Manchuria, so the hunting was much better than it had been in early 1951. By the time Jabara's second tour came to an end, he had become a triple ace with 15 confirmed kills. This made him the second-highest scoring Sabre pilot of the Korean War.

By 1966 Jabara was the youngest full colonel in the USAF at just 43 years of age. Boss of the F-100 Super Sabre-equipped 31st Tactical Fighter Wing, and slated for a combat tour in Vietnam, he was killed in a car accident on 17 November 1966. Both he and his daughter (who was driving the vehicle at the time) died in the crash, and they were buried at Arlington Cemetery in a single grave.

F-86A-5 Sabre 48-259 of Capt James Jabara, 334th FIS/4th FIG, Suwon, May 1951
Seen in early 4th FIG colours, this machine was one of a string of Sabres used by James Jabara during his first tour in Korea, which lasted from December 1950 through to 20 May 1951. One of the oldest F-86s to see combat in the war, this aircraft was actually Jabara's assigned jet, although it appears that he never actually scored a kill while flying it. Transferred to the 336th FIS following its pilot's hasty departure home, 48-259 was lost on 9 November 1951 when it suffered engine failure during a mission. Its pilot, Lt Freeland, ejected successfully and was recovered.

SPECIFICATION

North American F-86 Sabre

TYPE: jet fighter-bomber

ACCOMMODATION: pilot

DIMENSIONS: (for F-86F)
length 37 ft 6 in (11.43 m)
wingspan 39 ft 1 in (11.9 m)
height 14 ft 8.75 in (4.47 m)

WEIGHTS: empty 11,125 lb (5045 kg)
maximum take-off 20,611 lb (9350 kg)

PERFORMANCE: maximum speed 678 mph (1091 kmh)
range 850 miles (1368 km) with external tanks
powerplant General Electric J47-GE-27 (F-86F)
output 5970 lb st (26.56 kN)

ARMAMENT: six Colt-Browning 0.5-in machine guns in forward fuselage sides

FIRST FLIGHT DATE: 27 November 1946

OPERATORS: USA, UK, RAAF, SAAF, Japan, Norway, Pakistan, South Korea, Spain, West Germany, Canada

PRODUCTION: 9502

Aside from the Bell UH-1 Huey, no other post-war Western combat aircraft has been built in as great a numbers as the F-86. Total production amounted to 9502 airframes, covering no less than 13 separate land- and sea-based variants. The first contracts for the fighter were placed jointly by the USAAF and the US Navy in 1944, although the initial design featured unswept wings and a fuselage of greater diameter to allow it to house the Allison J35-2 engine. Following examination of captured German jet aircraft and related documentation, North American radically altered the design's shape. The revised XP-86 was a vastly superior machine, setting a new world speed record in 1949 thanks to the aerodynamic overhaul of its fuselage and incorporation of the all new GE J47 turbojet. F-86A Sabres were thrust into battle over Korea in December 1950, where the aircraft soon achieved the status of 'ace maker' in pitched battles against the MiG-15. Combat ushered in further improvements to the aircraft, while the radar-equipped F-86D also enjoyed widespread use with Air Defense Command as its first all-weather interceptor. A dynasty of Navy fighters in the form of the FJ-2/3 and -4 also served the fleet well into the late 1950s. Examples of the F-86 remained in the active inventory of a number of air forces into the early 1990s.

KURNASS

'The hunters became the hunted, and soon the first MiG-21 went down.'

At noon on 30 July 1970, four Israeli Defence Force/Air Force (IDF/AF) four-ship fighter formations ambushed Soviet MiG-21s operating over Egypt. The 'bait' for this engagement was provided by four Mirage IIIs imitating the flight profile of a high-altitude reconnaissance mission. Two four-ship combat air patrols (CAPs) lurking at low altitude below the coverage of Egyptian radar represented the main force to spring the trap, while a fourth formation of four was on immediate readiness at Refidim air base, in Sinai. Each formation was comprised of proven MiG killers drawn from different squadrons, for this was no ordinary mission.

The objective was to shoot down as many MiGs as possible, which is why only the best pilots were selected to participate in what was considered a team effort. Indeed, many of the pilots flying as wingmen were leaders in the own units, as well as being MiG killers.

The contribution of the IDF/AF F-4E Kurnass (Hebrew for Sledgehammer) force to this effort was a No 69 Sqn four-ship formation led by unit CO Avihu Ben-Nun and his navigator Shaul Levi. On his wing flew Aviem Sella and navigator Reuven Reshef. Both pilots were already MiG killers, although their navigators were not. Ben-Nun had been credited with two victories flying a Mirage III while Sella had claimed the second Kurnass kill on 8 February 1970. Now they were flying as one of the mission's two main CAPs.

The ruse worked well. Expecting to engage two unarmed reconnaissance Mirage IIIs flying straight and level at high altitude, the Soviet MiG-21 pilots actually met four fully armed delta fighters. The hunters became the hunted, and soon the first MiG-21 went down. Its pilot ejected, and instead of free-falling from high altitude and then opening his parachute, the Russian's canopy unfurled just seconds after he had left his fighter.

Descending slowly earthwards as the engagement was played out around him, the MiG-21 pilot acted as a 'beacon' for the Israelis.

Maj Gen Avihu Ben-Nun commanded the IDF/AF between 1987 and 1992. He is seen here prior to performing a flight in a Kurnass in November 1987 (*via Shlomo Aloni*)

Avihu Ben-Nun, with navigator Zvi Edan (Kesler), shot down a Syrian Su-7 in Kurnass 183 on 9 September 1972. It was to be the first of only five Su-7 kills credited to Kurnass aircrews, and the second victory scored in 183 (*via Shlomo Aloni*)

Ten IDF/AF aircrews attended the 4452nd TFTS's F-4 conversion course at George AFB, California, in March 1969. Seen here, standing, from left to right, are Ehud Henkin, Shaul Levi, Yair David, Rami Harpaz, Shamuel Hetz, Achikar Eyal, Avihu Ben-Nun, Menachem Eini, Yitzak Peer and Yoram Agmon. Henkin, Hetz and Levi would be killed in action while flying the aircraft, and four of these men had become PoWs within 12 months of this photograph being taken. The personnel in the front row are all USAF instructors (*via Shlomo Aloni*)

Whenever a pilot had to indicate his position during the combat, he would report, 'five miles south of the parachutist'.

It is generally accepted that four four-ship Soviet MiG-21 formations were scrambled to engage the Israeli 'reconnaissance' mission, and that they approached the air combat sector after the remaining main force CAPs were vectored to engage. One of the Mirage IIIs suffered a technical malfunction and had to abort the mission, the leader escorting him to Refidim, from where the readiness pilots were scrambled as a substitute.

In the ensuing air combat, Ben-Nun and Sella each shot down a MiG-21, the former, in Kurnass 105, chasing a MiG-21 which was flying west towards the Nile Valley at low altitude. First they launched an AIM-9 Sidewinder, which failed to even slow the MiG down despite exploding near to the target. Levi then achieved a radar lock on the MiG and Ben-Nun launched an AIM-7 Sparrow, which shot the jet down. The pilot failed to eject from his fighter.

When Ben-Nun and Sella regrouped, the latter noticed the two missing air-to-air missiles, and he asked Ben-Nun which weapon he had used to down the MiG-21. At that time the Sella family's pet was a dog called 'Sparrow', so Ben-Nun replied, 'With your dog'!

In the summer of 1989, 20 years after the first F-4 Kurnass had arrived in Israel on 5 September 1969, the survivors of the first conversion course gathered at Hatzor to repeat their 1969 group photograph at St Louis. Gaps were left for those crews who had been killed, the line up including (from left to right) a space for Ehud Henkin (killed in action on 7 October 1973), Yitzak Peer (retired with the rank of lieutenant colonel in 1984), Rami Harpaz (retired as a colonel), Yoram Agmon (retired as a brigadier general in 1983), Menachem Eini (retired from IDF/AF service as a brigadier general in 1983), a space for Shamuel Hetz (killed in action on 18 July 1970), Avihu Ben-Nun (IDF/AF CO 1987-92), a space for Shaul Levi (killed in action on 7 October 1973), Yair David and Achikar Eyal (retired as a lieutenant colonel in 1977). In the background is the first Kurnass to arrive in Israel (then numbered 01, later 601 and finally 101) (*via Shlomo Aloni*)

PILOT BIOGRAPHY – AVIHU BEN-NUN

Born in 1939, Avihu Ben-Nun joined the IDF at the age of 18 as required by Israeli Compulsory Military Service Law. He volunteered for the IDF/AF Flying School and duly trained as a fighter pilot, graduating in Class 29 on 19 November 1959. Having completed the fast jet conversion course at the Ouragan operational training unit, Ben-Nun then saw squadron service with the Mystere. He continued to fly the French fighter as a frontline Emergency Pilot (EP) during his subsequent reassignment to the Flying School as an instructor. In 1964 he returned to squadron service, flying the Shahak (Mirage III) with No 119 Sqn.

Shortly after the June 1967 Six Day War – during which Ben-Nun was the Senior Deputy Commander of Mystere-equipped No 116 Sqn – he was transferred to No 119 Sqn as Senior Deputy Commander. He marked his return to Shahaks with two Egyptian MiG-21 kills on 8 July and 10 October 1967.

In 1969 Ben-Nun was selected to form No 69 Sqn, which was the IDF/AF's second Kurnass (Phantom II) unit. He led the squadron until 1972, and was credited with his third kill (a Soviet MiG-21) on 30 July 1970. Becoming a staff officer following his departure from No 69 Sqn, Ben-Nun still saw regular combat in the unit's Kurnass as an EP. Indeed, he was credited with his fourth, and last, kill (a Syrian Su-7) on 9 September 1972 soon after leaving No 69 Sqn. Ben-Nun also flew eight missions during the October 1973 Yom Kippur War.

A leader from birth, Ben-Nun was promoted to full colonel in 1975 as head of the IDF/AF's Operations Department, and then served as Hatzor air base commander between 1977 and 1979. Promoted to brigadier general, Ben-Nun duly commanded Tel-Nof air base until 1982, when he became head of the Air Group and then IDF/AF Chief of Staff. Ben-Nun's assignment to the IDF Staff as Head of Planning, with the rank of major general, between June 1985 and July 1987 proved to be the stepping-stone which led to him being made IDF/AF commander between 22 September 1987 and 2 January 1992, when Ben-Nun finally retired. By then he had flown some 5000 hours, mostly in combat aircraft, and completed 450 operational sorties, during which he had claimed four kills.

Having set himself up as a private businessman following his distinguished career, Ben-Nun served for a number of years as the President of the No 69 Sqn Association, and he is presently the President of the Israeli Air Force Association.

Kurnass 183 of No 69 Sqn, Ramat David, 9 September 1972
The first Kurnass Su-7 kill was achieved by No 69 Sqn's former CO Avihu Ben-Nun (and his navigator Zvi Kesler), who was by then flying with the unit as an emergency posting pilot, in Kurnass 183. Ben-Nun was credited with four kills, two of which were scored in the Mirage III in 1967 and the remaining pair as a Kurnass pilot in 1970 and 1972. Ben-Nun graduated from fighter school class 29 in November 1959 and commanded No 69 Sqn between October 1969 and April 1972. He was then CO of Hatzor air base from 1977 to 1979 and Tel Nof from 1979 to 1982. After two IDF/AF staff assignments as Head of Air Group and Chief of Staff, Ben-Nun served as a member of the IDF Staff as Chief of Planning Branch, GHQ, between 6 June 1985 and 24 July 1987. On 22 September 1987 he succeeded Amos Lapidot as IDF/AF CO, leading the IDF/AF during the 1991 Gulf War, and completing his term on 2 January 1992.

SPECIFICATION

McDonnell Douglas F-4 Phantom II

(all dimensions and performance data for the F-4E)

TYPE:	all-weather jet interceptor
ACCOMMODATION:	two-man crew seated in tandem
DIMENSIONS:	(for F-4E) length 63 ft 0 in (19.20 m) wingspan 38 ft 4 in (11.68 m) height 16 ft 5 in (5.05 m)
WEIGHTS:	empty 30,328 lb (13,757 kg) maximum take-off 61,795 lb (28,030 kg)
PERFORMANCE:	maximum speed 1434 mph (2307 kmh) range 1613 miles (2596 km) ferry range powerplant two General Electric J79-GE-17 turbojets output 35,800 lb st (165 kN)
ARMAMENT:	One General Electric M61A1 20 mm rotary cannon in the nose; four AIM-7E-2 Sparrow missiles (intercept mission configuration) in underfuselage troughs; up to 16,000-lb (7258 kg) of external ordnance in various combinations
FIRST FLIGHT DATE:	27 May 1958
OPERATORS:	USA, UK, RAAF, Japan, Germany, South Korea, Spain, Egypt, Israel, Turkey, Greece, Iran
PRODUCTION:	5211

The most famous post-World War 2 fighter, the F-4 Phantom II is still very much a part of today's military scene, with examples being flown by nine air forces across the globe. However, this number is shrinking by the year, with most of the 5211 built during a 19-year production run having now been retired. Initially developed as a company private venture by McDonnell, the Phantom II evolved from an attack aircraft armed with four 20 mm cannon to an advanced, gunless, all-weather interceptor, boasting state-of-the-art radar and advanced missiles. Ordered by the US Navy for deployment aboard its carriers, the first production F-4Bs were delivered in December 1960. The following year a fly-off took place between a Navy Phantom II and various frontline USAF fighter types, with the results clearly showing that the F-4 was vastly superior to its Air Force contemporaries. The USAF immediately ordered the aircraft, and the jet went on to equip 16 of its 23 fighter wings within Tactical Air Command. The advent of the Vietnam War thrust the Phantom II into action, and the design's true multi-role capability soon saw it delivering tons of bombs in large-scale attack formations. Improved versions of the Phantom II (F-4E and F-4J) also made their debut in combat in the late 1960s.

ALERT NESHERS

'I opened fire and hit the empennage. The MiG lost control, its braking 'chute was deployed, and when it was nearly vertical, pointing downwards, the pilot ejected.'

On the evening of 17 October 1973, six Israeli Defence Force/Air Force fighter pilots arrived at Refidim, in Sinai, to take over responsibility for keeping a force of Nesher fighters on alert at this forward air base. Avraham Salmon, Dror Harish and Gidon Livni were from No 101 Sqn, while Moshe Hertz, Gidon Dror and Ra'anan Yosef were No 113 Sqn pilots. Hertz was the latter unit's senior deputy CO, while Livni was No 101's reconnaissance officer. Yosef was a No 113 Sqn emergency posting pilot, and Salmon, Harish and Dror were reserve pilots. All were seasoned combat veterans, and between them they boasted a combined score of 22.5 kills. Salmon and Harish were aces, Dror, Hertz and Livni were on their way and young Yosef would probably have joined this elite 'club' had he been in combat longer.

On 18 October the detachment was active as usual, with Salmon and Dror intercepting Egyptian MiG-17s at noon. Dror reported;

'We arrived over the bridgehead before the attackers. We turned through 360 degrees and then saw a four-ship formation of MiG-17s diving from south to north towards the bridges. "Avrahamik" chased the left-hand MiG, but I saw another four-ship formation trailing behind the first. I manoeuvred behind the trailing one, so there were nine aircraft ahead of me – two

Ra'anan Yosef signs a Nesher logbook during the Yom Kippur War. A graduate of IDF/AF Flying School Class 62 in July 1970, Yosef flew delta-fighters between 1971 and 1985, and was credited with three kills in 1973. (*via Shlomo Aloni*)

Delivered to No 101 Sqn in 1971, Nesher 10 was credited with at least seven kills, including two credited to Yosef – the first on 18 October and the second 24 hours later (*via Shlomo Aloni*)

MiG-17 four-ship formations and "Avrahamik" in between them. I chased the right-hand MiG in the trailing formation and shot it down with a Shafrir 2 missile. I then manoeuvred behind the remaining three MiGs of the trailing formation, my intention being to use my cannon to shoot down as many as possible. Then "Avrahamik" called for help. The explosion of the second MiG that I had shot down showered the canopy of his Nesher with debris and he could barely see anything. I led him back to a safe landing at Refidim. Six MiGs also returned home safely.'

The alert Neshers at Refidim were in action again in the afternoon, protecting the Israeli bridgehead from Egyptian air strikes. In a multi-bogey engagement, Hertz and Livni, with Harish and Yosef, shot down two MiG-17s and five MiG-21s. Two of the kills were among the most spectacular ever captured by the delta-fighter's gunsight cameras. Flying Nesher 09, Gidon Livni downed a MiG-21 crossing from left to right in front of him, while Nesher 10, flown by Ra'anan Yosef, destroyed a MiG-21, the gun-sight camera catching it with its braking 'chute deployed – the subject of this artwork.

'The attacking MiG-17s and escorting MiG-21s arrived as an armada', Yosef later reported. 'I immediately followed a pair of MiG-21s flying in close formation. One "stitch" and I was behind the trailing MiG. I opened fire and hit the empennage. The MiG lost control, its braking 'chute was deployed, and when it was nearly vertical, pointing downwards, the pilot ejected.'

Flying Nesher 10 from Refidim, Ra`anan Yosef was credited with his third, and last, kill on 19 October when he shot down this Egyptian MiG-21, whose braking-chute deployed possibly as a result of the damage inflicted by the burst of cannon fire from the Israeli jet. The starboard horizontal stabiliser also seems to have been badly damaged. Seconds later the Egyptian pilot ejected (*via Shlomo Aloni*)

PILOT BIOGRAPHY – RA'ANAN YOSEF

Born in 1949, Ra'anan Yosef joined the IDF at 18 as required by Israeli Compulsory Military Service Law. He volunteered for the IDF/AF Flying School (FS), where he trained as a fighter pilot. Yosef undertook his training shortly after the Six Day War, when the fighter course was seen to be the most prestigious military assignment in Israel. He graduated with Class 62 on 16 July 1970, less than a month before the Attrition War came to an end.

Assigned to No 113 Sqn's fighter pilots' Operational Training Unit (OTU) Course, Yosef trained on the Ouragan from August through to November 1970. He was then assigned to No 105 Sqn, where he flew both Super Mystere B 2s (SMB 2) and the locally-upgraded Sa'ar – an SMB 2 re-engined with a Pratt & Whitney J52 turbojet.

In early 1971 Yosef began his conversion onto the Shahak (Mirage III), having had just eight months of fast jet experience – four months in an Ouragan OTU and four months flying the SMB 2 and Sa'ar. Piloting the IDF/AF's premier interceptor with No 101 Sqn, Yosef was a regular squadron pilot until December 1972, when he was assigned to the Flying School to complete an Instructor's Course. His squadron status then changed, as he went from being a regular pilot to an Emergency Posting (EP) pilot, flying the Shahak one day a week.

With tension rising just prior to the outbreak of the October 1973 Yom Kippur War, the EP aircrews were ordered to join their squadrons on a full-time basis. Yosef flew just a single operational mission with No 101 Sqn before being transferred to No 113 Sqn, which was short of experienced fighter pilots following its recent transition onto the Nesher. Yosef completed an astounding 41 operational missions between 6 and 24 October, as well as two ferry flights and a single test flight! Flying as a wingman throughout the war, Yosef participated in five aerial combats and was credited with three confirmed kills.

Retiring from the IDF/AF in 1975 after completing his five years' service commitment, Yosef subsequently flew the Nesher and then the Kfir as a reserve pilot until 1985.

SPECIFICATION

IAI Nesher

TYPE:	jet fighter-bomber
ACCOMMODATION:	pilot
DIMENSIONS:	length 51 ft 0.5 in (15.56 m) wingspan 26 ft 11.5 in (8.22 m) height 13 ft 11.5 in (4,25 m)
WEIGHTS:	empty 15,763 lb (7150 kg) maximum take-off 30,200 lb (13,700 kg)
PERFORMANCE:	maximum speed 1451 mph (2335 kmh) range 777 miles (1250 km) with external tanks powerplant IAI Bedek Aviation Division-built SNECMA Atar 09C output 13,670 lb st (61 kN)
ARMAMENT:	Two DEFA 30 mm cannon in underfuselage; two Rafael Shafrir or AIM-9 Sidewinder missiles; provision for up to 4000-lb (1814 kg) of external ordnance in various combinations
FIRST FLIGHT DATE:	21 March 1971
OPERATORS:	Israel, Argentina
PRODUCTION:	61

Effectively a Mirage 5 built by Israeli Aircraft Industries without the benefit of a manufacturing licence, the Nesher differed from the Dassault product only in having a Martin-Baker JM 6 zero-zero ejection seat, some Israeli-developed avionics and internal wiring that allowed the aircraft to carry either the home-grown Rafael Shafrir or the AIM-9 Sidewinder. The first of 61 Neshers was handed over to the IDF/AF in 1971. Initial deliveries augmented the strength of the Mirage III-equipped Nos 101 and 117 Sqns, but the side-by-side operation of the two types resulted in unfair comparisons being made. The Nesher was heavier, with a higher fuel fraction, so no mixed formations were flown as it was thought that the Mirage III pilots would have to disengage from combat before the Neshers. The Nesher was also a better fighter-bomber, and in a mixed formation on an air-to-ground mission, the Mirage III's presence would be a handicap. Surprisingly, Nesher pilots were unable to exploit all their advantages against the older Mirage IIIs in dissimilar air combat training, where agility and manoeuvrability counted. Such training sessions ended when one of the participants reached bingo fuel. Frustrated pilots immediately preferred the Mirage III, but in combat the differences between the Nesher and the original delta fighter did not seem that significant, although the Nesher's better combat endurance was of great importance. Replaced in frontline service by the Kfir, most surviving Neshers were refurbished by IAI and sold to Argentina as Daggers between 1978 and 1982.

Nesher 61 of Giora Epstein, No 113 Sqn, Hatzor air base, 20 October 1973

Although a No 101 Sqn pilot, Epstein downed eight aircraft while flying No 113 Sqn's Nesher 61. This aircraft was also flown by Ra'anan Yosef on five combat missions between 9 and 23 October 1973, although unlike Epstein, he did not claim any victories with it.

APPENDICES
AIRCRAFT OF THE ACES

Titles published to date

AIRCRAFT OF THE ACES 1
• MUSTANG ACES OF THE EIGHTH
AIR FORCE • ISBN 1 85532 447 4

AIRCRAFT OF THE ACES 2 • Bf 109
ACES OF NORTH AFRICA AND THE
MEDITERRANEAN • ISBN 1 85532 448 2

AIRCRAFT OF THE ACES 3
• WILDCAT ACES OF WORLD WAR 2
• ISBN 1 85532 486 5

AIRCRAFT OF THE ACES 4
• KOREAN WAR ACES
• ISBN 1 85532 501 2

AIRCRAFT OF THE ACES 5 • LATE
MARQUE SPITFIRE ACES 1942–45
• ISBN 1 85532 575 6

AIRCRAFT OF THE ACES 6 • FOCKE-WULF
Fw 190 ACES OF THE RUSSIAN FRONT
• ISBN 1 85532 518 7

AIRCRAFT OF THE-ACES 7 • MUSTANG
ACES OF THE NINTH & 15TH AIR FORCES
& THE RAF • ISBN 1 85532 583 7

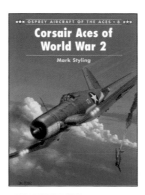

AIRCRAFT OF THE ACES 8
• CORSAIR ACES OF WORLD WAR 2
• ISBN 1 85532 530 6

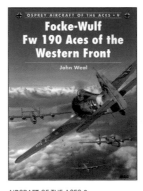

AIRCRAFT OF THE ACES 9
• FOCKE-WULF Fw 190 ACES OF THE
WESTERN FRONT • ISBN 1 85532 595 0

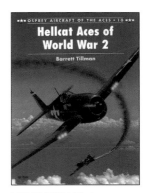

AIRCRAFT OF THE ACES 10
• HELLCAT ACES OF WORLD WAR 2
• ISBN 1 85532 596 9

AIRCRAFT OF THE ACES 11
• Bf109D/E ACES 1939-41
• ISBN 1 85532 487 3

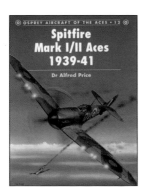

AIRCRAFT OF THE ACES 12
• SPITFIRE MARK I/II ACES 1939-41
• ISBN 1 85532 627 2

AIRCRAFT OF THE ACES 13
• JAPANESE ARMY AIR FORCE ACES
1937-45 • ISBN 1 85532 529 2

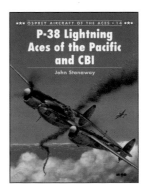

AIRCRAFT OF THE ACES 14
• P-38 LIGHTNING ACES OF THE PACIFIC
AND CBI • ISBN 1 85532 633 7

AIRCRAFT OF THE ACES 15
• SOVIET ACES OF WORLD WAR 2
• ISBN 1 85532 632 9

AIRCRAFT OF THE ACES 16
• SPITFIRE MARK V ACES 1941-45
• ISBN 1 85532 635 3

AIRCRAFT OF THE ACES 17
• GERMAN JET ACES OF WORLD WAR 2
• ISBN 1 85532 634 5

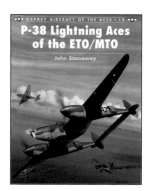

AIRCRAFT OF THE ACES 18
• HURRICANE ACES 1939-40
• ISBN 1 85532 597 7

AIRCRAFT OF THE ACES 19
• P-38 LIGHTNING ACES OF THE
ETO/MTO • ISBN 1 85532 698 1

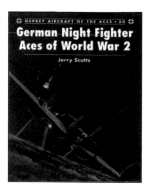

AIRCRAFT OF THE ACES 20
• GERMAN NIGHT FIGHTER ACES OF
WORLD WAR 2 • ISBN 1 85532 696 5

AIRCRAFT OF THE ACES 21
• POLISH ACES OF WORLD WAR 2
• ISBN 1 85532 726 0

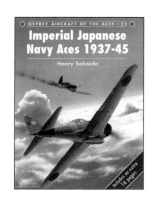

AIRCRAFT OF THE ACES 22
• IMPERIAL JAPANESE NAVY ACES
1937-45 • ISBN 1 85532 727 9

AIRCRAFT OF THE ACES 23
• FINNISH ACES OF WORLD WAR 2
• ISBN 1 85532 783 X

AIRCRAFT OF THE ACES 24
• P-47 THUNDERBOLT ACES OF THE
EIGHTH AIR FORCE • ISBN 1 85532 729 5

AIRCRAFT OF THE ACES 25
• MESSERSCHMITT Bf 110 *ZERSTÖRER*
ACES OF WORLD WAR 2
• ISBN 1 85532 753 8

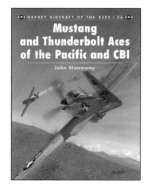

AIRCRAFT OF THE ACES 26 • MUSTANG
AND THUNDERBOLT ACES OF THE
PACIFIC AND CBI • ISBN 1 85532 780 5

AIRCRAFT OF THE ACES 27
• TYPHOON AND TEMPEST ACES OF
WORLD WAR 2 • ISBN 1 85532 779 1

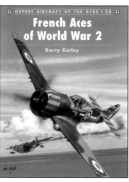

AIRCRAFT OF THE ACES 28
• FRENCH ACES OF WORLD WAR 2
• ISBN 1 85532 898 4

AIRCRAFT OF THE ACES 29
• Bf 109F/G/K ACES OF THE WESTERN
FRONT • ISBN 1 85532 905 0

AIRCRAFT OF THE ACES 30 • P-47
THUNDERBOLT ACES OF THE NINTH AND
FIFTEENTH AIR FORCES • ISBN 1 85532 906 9

AIRCRAFT OF THE ACES 31 (SPECIAL)
• VIII FIGHTER COMMAND AT WAR
'LONG REACH' • ISBN 1 85532 907 7

AIRCRAFT OF THE ACES 32
• ALBATROS ACES OF WORLD WAR 1
• ISBN 1 85532 960 3

AIRCRAFT OF THE ACES 33
• NIEUPORT ACES OF WORLD WAR 1
• ISBN 1 85532 961 1

AIRCRAFT OF THE ACES 34
• ITALIAN ACES OF WORLD WAR 2
• ISBN 1 84176 078 1

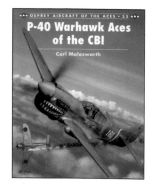

AIRCRAFT OF THE ACES 35
• P-40 WARHAWK ACES OF THE CBI
• ISBN 1 84176 079 X

AIRCRAFT OF THE ACES 36
• P-39 AIRACOBRA ACES OF WORLD WAR 2 • ISBN 1 84176 204 0

AIRCRAFT OF THE ACES 37
• Bf 109 ACES OF THE RUSSIAN FRONT • ISBN 1 84176 084 6

AIRCRAFT OF THE ACES 38
• TOMAHAWK AND KITTYHAWK ACES OF THE RAF AND COMMONWEALTH • ISBN 1 84176 083 8

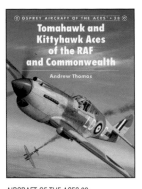

AIRCRAFT OF THE ACES 39
• SPAD VII ACES OF WORLD WAR 1 • ISBN 1 84176 222 9

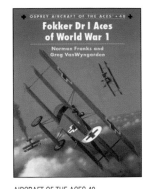

AIRCRAFT OF THE ACES 40
• FOKKER Dr I ACES OF WORLD WAR 1 • ISBN 1 84176 223 7

AIRCRAFT OF THE ACES 41 • AMERICAN VOLUNTEER GROUP COLOURS AND MARKINGS • ISBN 1 84176 224 5

AIRCRAFT OF THE ACES 42
• AMERICAN ACES OF WORLD WAR 1 • ISBN 1 84176 375 6

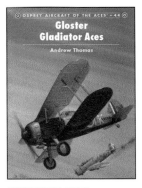

AIRCRAFT OF THE ACES 43
• P-40 WARHAWK ACES OF THE MTO • ISBN 1 84176 288 1

AIRCRAFT OF THE ACES 44
• GLOSTER GLADIATOR ACES • ISBN 1 84176 289 X

AIRCRAFT OF THE ACES 45
• BRITISH AND EMPIRE ACES OF WORLD WAR 1 • ISBN 1 84176 377 2

AIRCRAFT OF THE ACES 46
• AUSTRO-HUNGARIAN ACES OF WORLD WAR 1 • ISBN 1 84176 376 4

AIRCRAFT OF THE ACES 47
• SPAD XII/XIII ACES OF WORLD WAR 1 • ISBN 1 84176 316 0

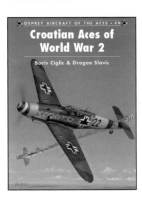

AIRCRAFT OF THE ACES 48
• DOLPHIN AND SNIPE ACES OF WORLD WAR 1 • ISBN 1 84176 317 9

AIRCRAFT OF THE ACES 49
• CROATIAN ACES OF WORLD WAR 2 • ISBN 1 84176 435 3

AIRCRAFT OF THE ACES 50
• HUNGARIAN ACES OF WORLD WAR 2 • ISBN 1 84176 436 1

AIRCRAFT OF THE ACES 51 (SPECIAL)
• 'DOWN TO EARTH' STRAFING ACES OF THE EIGHTH AIR FORCE
• ISBN 1 84176 437 X

AIRCRAFT OF THE ACES 52
• SOPWITH CAMEL ACES OF WORLD WAR 1 • ISBN 1 84176 534 1

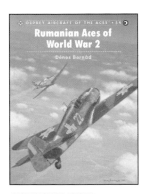

AIRCRAFT OF THE ACES 53
• FOKKER D VII ACES OF WORLD WAR 1 PART 1 • ISBN 1 84176 533 3

AIRCRAFT OF THE ACES 54
• RUMANIAN ACES OF WORLD WAR 2 • ISBN 1 84176 535 X

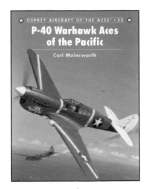

AIRCRAFT OF THE ACES 55
• P-40 WARHAWK ACES OF THE PACIFIC • ISBN 1 84176 536 8

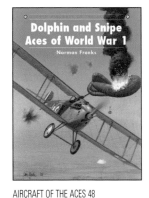

AIRCRAFT OF THE ACES 56
• LaGG & LAVOCHKIN ACES OF WORLD
WAR 2 • ISBN 1 84176 609 7

AIRCRAFT OF THE ACES 57
• HURRICANE ACES 1941-45
• ISBN 1 84176 610 0

AIRCRAFT OF THE ACES 58
• SLOVAKIAN AND BULGARIAN ACES OF
WORLD WAR 2 • ISBN 1 84176 652 6

AIRCRAFT OF THE ACES 59
• ISRAELI MIRAGE AND NESHER ACES
• ISBN 1 84176 653 4

AIRCRAFT OF THE ACES 60
• ISRAELI F-4 PHANTOM II ACES
• ISBN 1 84176 783 2

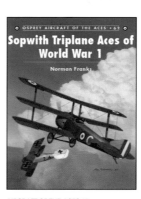

AIRCRAFT OF THE ACES 61 (SPECIAL)
• 'TWELVE TO ONE' V FIGHTER
COMMAND ACES OF THE PACIFIC
• ISBN 1 84176 784 0

AIRCRAFT OF THE ACES 62
• SOPWITH TRIPLANE ACES OF WORLD
WAR 1 • ISBN 1 84176 728 X

AIRCRAFT OF THE ACES 63
• FOKKER D VII ACES OF WORLD WAR 1
PART 2 • ISBN 1 84176 729 8

INDEX